THE LEGACY OF
THE RYUKYU KINGDOM

THE LEGACY OF THE RYUKYU KINGDOM
An Okinawan History

Written by
TAKARA Kurayoshi
Translated by Lina Terrell

Japan Publishing Industry Foundation for Culture

Publisher's Note
This book follows the Hepburn system of romanization, with long vowels indicated by macrons. The tradition of placing the family name first has been followed for Japanese, Chinese, and Korean names. There is no standard system of romanization for the Okinawan language. The most used or verifiable spelling has been utilized for Okinawan terms.

The Legacy of the Ryukyu Kingdom: An Okinawan History
Takara Kurayoshi.
Translated by Lina Terrell.

Published by
Japan Publishing Industry Foundation for Culture (JPIC)
2-2-30 Kanda-Jinbocho, Chiyoda-ku, Tokyo 101-0051, Japan

First English edition: March 2025

© 1993 Takara Kurayoshi
English translation © 2025 Japan Publishing Industry Foundation for Culture
All rights reserved

This publication is the result of a collaborative effort between the Japan Institute of International Affairs (JIIA) and Japan Publishing Industry Foundation for Culture (JPIC).

This book is a translation of *Ryūkyū Ōkoku* (Iwanami Shoten, Publishers, Tokyo, 1993). English publishing rights arranged with Iwanami Shoten, Publishers, Tokyo.

Book design: Cecilia Rodríguez Guzmán
Jacket and cover photo: Courtesy of CEphoto, Uwe Aranas

Printed in Japan
hardcover ISBN 978-4-86658-258-0
ebook (ePub) ISBN 978-4-86658-259-7
ebook (PDF) ISBN 978-4-86658-260-3
https://www.jpicinternational.com/

Contents

Foreword		7
Preface to the English Edition		11
Introduction		13
CHAPTER I	**Discovering the Kingdom**	23
	1. The Pioneer of Okinawan Studies	24
	2. Kawakami Hajime's Careless Words	27
	3. The Origin of Uniqueness	34
CHAPTER II	**Ancient Ryukyu**	39
	1. The Period of Transformation Begins	40
	2. The Road to the Kingdom	47
	3. The Era of King Shō Shin: Establishment of the Kingdom	59
	4. Toward an Era of Change	70
CHAPTER III	**Ryukyu in Asia**	77
	1. The Theater of Engagement	78
	2. Characteristics of Overseas Trade	86
	3. In Search of Possible Ryukyuan History	104
CHAPTER IV	**The Kingdom of Writs**	111
	1. Rediscovery	112
	2. What Is Reflected?	116
	3. What the Document Format Reveals	123

CHAPTER V	**The Organization of the Kingdom**	133
	1. Various Officials	134
	2. What Were *Hiki*?	145
	3. The Military Defense Structure and the *Kōri-Hiki* System	154

Conclusion — 162
   1. What Ancient Ryukyu Represents — 162
   2. For the Sake of Restoration — 168

Postscript — 175

Historical Timeline for Ryukyu/Okinawa — 177

Key References — 187

About the Author and Translator — 189

Foreword

The Legacy of the Ryukyu Kingdom was originally published in 1993 by Iwanami Shoten as part of its *Shinsho* ("new book") series. When this series began in 1938, Japan was heading towards World War II and under a strict speech control policy. Despite this beginning, the series has persisted in advocating academic freedom and scientific development, nurturing a rich culture and education without being overwhelmed by current events. It continues to serve as a meeting place for readers and scholarship across generations. For any reader venturing into unfamiliar academic territory, it's no exaggeration to say that this series is a great place to start.

Along these lines, my own first encounter with the kingdom of Ryukyu was undoubtedly through this book. The meeting, whether fate or coincidence, occurred during my third year of high school and it inspired me to jump into the field of Ryukyuan history. At the time, even local bookstores in Okinawa had few, if any, books on the topic of the Ryukyu Kingdom; instead, most book titles referred only to the "history of Okinawa." I remember clearly how the four characters for "Ryukyu Kingdom" on one book leapt out from the row of bright red covers of the *Shinsho* series. I later enrolled at the University of the Ryukyus with the intent of studying Ryukyuan history. During my entrance examinations, Professor Takara Kurayoshi, the author of this book, presided over the large team of interviewers.

Takara Kurayoshi was born in 1947 on Izena Island, Okinawa Prefecture, the birthplace of Shō En, founder of the Second Shō dynasty. After graduating from Aichi University of Education in 1971, he served as director of the Okinawa Historical Materials Editorial Office and Urasoe City Library before obtaining his doctoral degree in 1993 with his paper "Fundamental Research on the History of the Ryukyu Kingdom." After retiring as a professor from the Faculty of Law and Letters at the University of the Ryukyus, he served as vice governor of Okinawa Prefecture and currently holds the title of professor emeritus. As a specialist in Ryukyuan history, he has authored numerous works, including *Ryūkyū no jidai* (The Age of Ryukyu) [Chikuma Shobō, 2012], all of which seek to puzzle out the structure of the Ryukyu Kingdom. Professor Takara is well known for having taken on an extraordinary workload compared to most typical university professors. Particularly noteworthy are his indispensable contributions as a historical consultant for NHK's first historical drama based in Ryukyuan history, *Ryūkyū no kaze* (Wind of the Ryukyu Islands), and his central role in the reconstruction of Shuri Castle.

This book comprises an introduction, five main chapters, and a conclusion. The introduction gives insight into his stance as a historian rooted in Okinawa as a field of study. While Okinawa contains the history of the Ryukyu Kingdom, the grim experience of the Battle of Okinawa somehow inevitably overshadows any other discussion. The difficulty of telling the history of Ryukyu in the face of such circumstances becomes apparent.

Chapter 1 introduces the figure in Okinawan studies most revered by Professor Takara: Ifa Fuyū, the father of Okinawan studies. During Ifa's lifetime, Okinawa suppressed its own history and moved towards integrating with Japan. During this period, in 1911, Kawakami Hajime visited Okinawa and delivered a lecture in which he stated, "Okinawa has a unique history distinct from Japan." However, he faced fierce criticism for this from Okinawan intellectuals at the time and soon departed Okinawa in great disappointment. In this we see an expression of the pain of Okinawans, after the collapse of the kingdom, as they closed away their own history in order to become Japanese, unable to take pride in Okinawa's unique history and culture. As this complicated sentiment built up, no doubt many Okinawans lost their direct connection with the history of Ryukyu; however, this changed completely during Professor Takara's tenure at the University of the Ryukyus. Indeed, a new era has dawned in which Okinawans eagerly embrace Ryukyuan history as the foundation of their Okinawan identity.

Chapters 2 and 3 vividly depict the "The Age of Great Trade," the dynamic historical period when the Ryukyu Kingdom developed its connections across the Asian world with its port of Naha at the flourishing center of the Maritime Silk Road.

The examination of the writs of appointment in Chapter 4, and of the *hiki* system for military organization in Chapter 5, are classic examples of Professor Takara's kingdom study projects. Chapter 4 is an outstanding and detailed analysis of official documents of appointment issued by the Ryukyu royal government, shedding new light on the royal government's structure from a very limited amount of text. Chapter 5 elucidates the *hiki* system, the military organization of the kingdom as deduced from official titles in the writs of appointment. The revelation that the kingdom's land-based system of service matched the organization of personnel aboard its trade ships illustrates the ways in which the kingdom period's government structured itself.

To borrow Professor Takara's words, we can think of this book as akin to an orchestral performance of various historical materials, harmonizing melodies from several sources to form a grand symphony playing a history of the Ryukyu Kingdom. His perspective on this history is always dynamic and filled with hope for the future.

Though thirty years have passed since the original publication of *The Legacy of the Ryukyu Kingdom*, it yields fresh insights with every read. For all its compactness as a *Shinsho* publication, this excellent book is a rare treasure for delving deeply into the internal structure of the Ryukyu Kingdom. Surely it will continue to flourish along with Okinawan society.

While the Ryukyu Kingdom is no more, Okinawa still carries the history and culture of that era. With the publication of this English translation, I am delighted that readers in the English-speaking world will be able to contemplate the history of this now-lost kingdom.

Finally, I wish to express my gratitude to the translator who was able to produce a translation that both clarifies many difficult specialized terms with the addition of explanations and annotations and manages to capture the spirit of the Ryukyu Kingdom era.

Okinawa University
Associate Professor
Maeda Shūko

Preface to the English Edition

Japan is composed of forty-seven regional administrative units stretching from Hokkaido in the north to Okinawa Prefecture in the south. Of course, each of these regional units has unique historical and cultural characteristics, but among them, Okinawa Prefecture at the southern end is known for its distinctive individuality.

Though the people of Okinawa share roots with Japan's mainland culture, they eventually embarked on their own history to establish an independent nation, the Ryukyu Kingdom, in 1429. From their central capital at Shuri Castle, they governed a territory of islands scattered across a vast stretch of ocean. Their distinctive culture developed as they actively engaged in trade with various Asian countries, especially China and Japan. In 1879, however, the kingdom was annexed by modern Japan and became Okinawa Prefecture.

Even then, a tumultuous history continued.

During the final decisive battle between Japan and the United States in the Pacific War, known as the Battle of Okinawa (1945), fierce ground battles resulted in enormous numbers of casualties. In addition to the one-in-four Okinawans who lost their lives, significant legacies from the Ryukyu Kingdom era were also lost. After World War II, Okinawa was removed from Japanese administration and placed under direct US rule. The United States valued Okinawa for its strategic location and constructed extensive military bases, resulting in the emergence of "Base Okinawa" that continues to this day.

The people of Okinawa persisted in seeking an end to US rule and a return to Japan. Although the conditions of this return were not as they had hoped, Okinawa Prefecture was restored on May 15, 1972.

PREFACE TO THE ENGLISH EDITION

Today, Okinawa is often thought of as an island fraught with base-related issues, or as a tourist resort endowed with unique culture and lovely seas. However, Okinawa is steeped in the history of the Ryukyu Kingdom. Knowing this background can deepen one's understanding of Okinawa.

This book is written to appeal to the general reader, focusing on the ancient Ryukyu era when the Ryukyu Kingdom emerged and engaged with the world in many ways.

I am delighted that my thoughts can reach even more people through this English translation.

Takara Kurayoshi

Introduction

Divine Consultations

"Next month, around 10 p.m. on the 17th, a goddess will descend from the moon at Kadena Air Force Base. I am begging you to save her. Please."

This was near the end of August 1987. A young man barely past twenty, his face serious, had come to me at the Okinawa Prefectural Museum to make his appeal. "Oh, my god, here we go again," I thought, inviting him to sit. I lit a cigarette and asked him why he thought I should perform this rescue. My question must have lit a spark, because the young man proceeded to talk nonstop for two hours. He finally left when I said, "Fine. I don't know that I have the power to save anybody, but come back here around 9 a.m. on the 18th of next month, and I will give you the full report."

Promises must be kept, so on the evening of the 17th, I drove up to Kadena Air Force Base and parked outside the main gate to wait for 10 o'clock. The moon was bright in a cloudless sky. I reclined my seat back as far as it would go and lay back, asking myself what I thought I was doing. I'd long gone past the point of smiling wryly and telling myself I was a good person. Remorse welled up, and I lay there watching the moon, struggling with my feelings. Finally, 10 o'clock came and went. Obviously, I saw no changes around the moon.

The next morning, the young man reappeared in my office at the museum. "I remained for two hours after the appointed time, but no goddess appeared," I reported. "Oh, I see," he said, desolate. And saying nothing more, he left with no hint of dissatisfaction on his face.

INTRODUCTION

A Historian's "Sense of the Field"

Readers may be wondering why I would start a book on the history of the Ryukyu Kingdom with such a strange little story. Bear with me for a moment, because my reason springs from my philosophical stance as a working historian doing research in Okinawa.

My encounter with the young man in the story above is not the only time I've done divine consulting. In fact, these odd conversations only grew more frequent as I became more well known as a scholar of Okinawan history. We can understand the former high school principal who asked me to reconstruct his family genealogy. "Our family records were destroyed in the war, and you are a historian," he said. "It's a lot to ask, but can't you help us restore them?" Then there was the elderly woman who forwarded a message to me, claiming she had been asked to do so by Shō Shin, king of the Ryukyu Kingdom at its peak in the sixteenth century. A woman whose son had been ill made the rounds to pray at several shrines on the advice of a shamaness asked me why this cured her son's illness when doctors had been unable to do anything for him. Another woman called to tell me that I should lead a giant prayer festival at a certain holy shrine, because the reason so many young people die in traffic accidents is that they don't worship properly at that shrine. My life is full of these kinds of conversations.

Why do I feel historians should be open to such conversations about the divine? It would be easy to simply dismiss these stories as stupid, or just chase the nutcases away. Or, I could smooth everything over by giving some suitable but vague answer that is easily accepted and lets them leave. But I think there are always serious, real questions behind these encounters. For example, how could I be indifferent to the plea of an eighty-year-old woman who came to me and said, "After the war ended, the Americans bulldozed the area where our family tomb was and built a base. So now I don't know where our tomb is. Before I die, I want you to help me find it. I want to go there and clasp my hands in prayer before I die." The fact is, I can't ignore such things, because then I would lose something important in my role as a historian. So, I've made it my responsibility to listen with attention to these requests for advice, taking them seriously and answering as best I can.

Before I consider myself a historian, I consider myself a modern person living in the here and now, and it is from this position that I wish to view and attempt to understand the modern world, so full of contradictions. This wish is close to my own prayer for understanding. By taking these questions seriously, I avoid making a mockery of them, and I am able to form a sense of my field of study, in order to better understand history.

In the Bar Districts

There was a time when I went out every evening to various bar districts. I went to places all over Okinawa, but I was an especially frequent visitor to the bars that developed around the American military bases.

After the Battle of Okinawa ended and vast American bases were built all over, Okinawa underwent rapid urbanization. Not only base workers (called "military workers"), but also people working in commercial and service industries for the GIs (American soldiers) poured in from rural farming regions and remote islands, creating "base towns" (instead of "temple towns") outside the gates of every military base. Examples include Koza (present-day Okinawa City), Kitamae in Chatan, Shinkaichi in Kin, and Henoko.

During those long Okinawa nights, I met a wide variety of people, and I heard many different stories. "I made so much money, it was like it was raining dollars," exclaimed one happy former bar owner. "Got married and had two kids, but the GI husband went off on what he said were 'training exercises' and never came back," said one woman, almost as if she were speaking of someone else. "Before payday, the GIs are poor too, and I can't tell you how many times I got taken on a free ride," laughed a former sex worker.

A half-American rock musician told me during a break after an intense performance, "It was rough during the Vietnam War. Slack off in playing and the GIs would throw beer bottles at us! That made for a bad vibe." He downed his beer with evident enjoyment, and continued. "From the stage, I could always tell which soldiers were headed out to Vietnam the next day. They were the ones sitting hunched in a corner, silently trying to drown themselves in drink. Seeing those guys always made me want to work harder to give them a good send-off."

I did not set out to investigate Okinawa's unknown postwar history. I just wanted to know more about these people who lived in close contact with the US military personnel in the postwar era. I wanted to sharpen my "sense of the field" by learning more about the people's interior landscape during that period, all with the hope of becoming a better Okinawan historian.

The people living their lives along the streets of base towns serving the US Army in the postwar era had many hard stories to share of that time. Depending on how one views it, the people who come to me for divine consultations may also be in their own unhappy situations, but they are the ones living in today's Okinawa. When I talk about the history of Okinawa, I have to keep in mind that history is filled with people who share that attitude with modern people, of just trying to live their lives in their own time. I want to emphasize this idea. It is one I make sure to stress to my students as well.

INTRODUCTION

In Front of the Youth

I have been teaching a course on Ryukyuan history at a local junior college since 1975. Most of my students are female college students. My full-time job as a civil servant means I teach only for half a year during the second semester and, moreover, my class has to be on Saturday afternoons when everyone is wanting to go out and have fun. Yet, surprisingly, every year applications for my classes exceed available space, indicating a strong interest in Ryukyuan history. This work has provided me with another opportunity to hone my "sense of the field."

I once used a survey to find out what my students were interested in studying. Many responses reflected my students' youth; one, however, caught my attention. The writer pointed out that the history they had heard about from their parents was always about the history of being bullied. "Why is Okinawa's history so dark? There must be other history that shows a more generous way of life. I want to know more about that."

The view of Okinawa as a victim in history has long been prevalent, sometimes reaching the level of ideology. And it is true that the Ryukyuan people were exploited like slaves under Satsuma's rule. A harsh poll tax imposed by the Shuri government resulted in miserable conditions for people in the remote islands of Miyako and Yaeyama. The Meiji government unilaterally ended the Ryukyu Kingdom with the "Disposition of Ryukyu,"[1] which in turn created Okinawa Prefecture, and allowed for no further discussion or protest. Despite their new status as equal Japanese citizens, Okinawans suffered discriminatory treatment by mainland Japanese because of their differ-

---

1. Also known as the Ryukyu Annexation or Annexation of Okinawa, the Disposition of Ryukyu was a political process that saw the absorption of the Ryukyu Kingdom into the Japanese empire as Okinawa Prefecture.

ent customs and traditions. Another bitter memory is the Battle of Okinawa, during which one in four Okinawans lost their lives due to vicious actions by supposedly "friendly forces" in the Japanese military. In the postwar era, under the direct rule of the US occupying forces, they were once again cut off from the rest of Japanese society and their human rights were ignored in the midst of harsh living conditions. Certainly, there is plenty of darkness and bullying in this history.

The Need for the Big Picture

Starting in elementary school and continuing through high school, young Okinawans repeatedly hear the story of the Battle of Okinawa in special lectures. June 23rd, the day the Battle of Okinawa ended, is Okinawa's Memorial Day (Irei no Hi, "day to console the spirits of the dead"). In preparation for that day, teachers commonly prepare special lectures to teach their students about the reality of the final months of the war and to value peace. I think this important work of dealing head-on with the Battle of Okinawa, and using these stories to foster in their students a love for peace and a hatred for war, is a credit to the teachers of Okinawa, and a tradition worth continuing. However, I find it concerning that so much focus is given to the Battle of Okinawa, and very little time is spent on the overall picture of Okinawa's history. There is no question that we must teach our children about the battle and its lessons. The Battle of Okinawa, however, is only one piece of Okinawa's history, and it seems to me that focusing solely on it means we end up equating that one terrible battle with the whole history of Okinawa.

At the start of every semester when I teach the Ryukyu history course, I give the students a short test to find out what they know already. I ask them to write a few words explaining a variety of historical terms such as "tributary ships," "poll tax," "mass suicide," and so on; perhaps as a result of those special classes, they show that they are often quite familiar with events related to the Battle of Okinawa. However, they leave blanks next to other terms, or just write that they have never heard of a term.

Rather than blaming school teachers for this situation, perhaps we should blame the historians for being ineffectual. Have these historians grasped the greater picture of Okinawa's history and adequately elucidated it? In order to increase interest in the full breadth of Okinawa's history, including the Battle of Okinawa, we must draw our focus away from the victim's lament of "darkness" and "bullying." For every part of our history, we must clearly present the dynamism of the people who took bold actions. Faced with young people who want to know more about the history of Ryukyu, I feel convinced that we need to clearly showcase the dynamism of the Okinawans who forged our history as they lived and worked in their own time.

The premodern era of Okinawa's history has been the least studied in the overall record. The thin, flat picture provided by old history books still prevails, with not enough fresh and ambitious work coming out. To build up a more complete picture, our premodern history needs a thorough reworking. We can talk all day about the importance of that complete picture of our history, but clearly, unless we do the work, such talk is meaningless.

Tracking Down Premodern History

To seriously engage with our premodern history, we need to increase the ranks of like-minded colleagues as well as the number of people who can read often difficult historical documents. The Okinawa History Research Society, of which I am the executive director, holds weekly meetings to read historical documents. We meet around a big conference table at the Okinawa Historical Materials Editorial Office, where I worked before moving to the Okinawa Prefectural Museum. We started with the relatively plentiful original documents from the early modern period. Our group was not limited to academic scholars, but was also joined by people from a variety of professions, including university students, civil servants, company employees, police officers, office assistants, and manga artists. Besides my goal of developing professional historians of premodern history through collaborative learning, I also believed we had to include the perspectives of ordinary people in our reading sessions. This group began its meetings in 1974 and continues to this day.

In the summer, we hold summer seminars in different locations. For example, we might travel to the outer islands and stay at guesthouses, where we discuss what kind of historical picture we can glean from our recent reading. A few members might present talks. Our debates over the material often continue late into the night. The field of history consists, in large part, of many scholars working independently to stitch together the facts picked from their readings of historical documents. The essential element in this process comes when these scholars then meet to deepen their individual understanding by sharing and discussing the meaning of their findings. We were perhaps fortunate in that no one among us was the expert with all the knowledge, so our meetings had a spontaneous and natural feel to them.

In addition, I made a point of visiting Okinawa's remote islands when I had the chance. I had heard many times that there were no premodern historical materials left after the Battle of Okinawa destroyed them all, but I wanted to see for myself whether this was true or not.

The results were quite a surprise. Though scant, there were, in fact, historical materials preserved in the outer islands. For example, when I visited Tarama Island in the Miyako group, I found records illustrating the daily realities of island administration from around the end of the early modern period, population registers with meticulous details

INTRODUCTION

on family composition, and blacksmithing reports. A visit to Izena Island yielded a late Tokugawa-era report of the program of activities for an annual public event hosted by the Shuri royal government. Upon visiting an old family residence in Nishihara on the main island of Okinawa, I found a handed-down collection of ancient papers describing how to perform rituals at sacred sites connected to the royal government. Finally, Ishigaki Island had a vast archive of materials dating from the early modern period with documents that completely revise our understanding of that period. Naturally, I took pictures of all of these materials, and we used them as texts for our study group.

In the process of finding and studying these materials, I feel I have learned two things. First, even though such materials are just objects to be studied for historians, in fact, in presenting directly to us the lives of real people, these documents are not merely inanimate objects. Secondly, the mental image of "Okinawa" based on a city like Naha is very different from the image that arises from a trip to the outer islands. Unexpectedly, Okinawa offers many variations of itself. The customs and traditions of the various islands, even the spoken dialects, all differ markedly. It might seem obvious but realizing Okinawa's depths felt like a fresh discovery to me.

It is no exaggeration to say that when I first set my goal of elucidating the history of Okinawa's premodern period, I had no knowledgeable authority on whom to rely, and no seniors to take me on as their apprentice. Instead, Okinawa itself became my teacher.

The work of premodern historical research relies on finding and explaining the hidden historical record to be found in the lives and minds of people living today, giving the research modern significance.

In this book, I will first take a closer look at two modern figures who faced difficulties in their attempts to gain insight into the Ryukyu Kingdom; and then outline the overall picture of the kingdom itself in its heyday, with a study of its internal state of affairs.

CHAPTER I
DISCOVERING THE KINGDOM

CHAPTER I

1. The Pioneer of Okinawan Studies

The Tomb of Ifa Fuyū

There was once a pioneering scholar who investigated the premodern history of Ryukyu from the perspective of the Okinawan people. His name was Ifa Fuyū.[1]

Whenever I feel my own determination as an Okinawan historian falter, I always pay a visit to the grave of my field's much-esteemed forebear. His grave is about a fifteen-minute walk from the Urasoe City Library, my current place of employment.

Affectionately known as the "father of Okinawan studies," Ifa was a scholar who took on every topic of Okinawan history. He was born into a wealthy family in Naha in 1876, just before the annexation of Ryukyu, and after studying at the Third Higher School in Kyoto (present-day Kyoto University), studied linguistics at Tokyo Imperial University (now University of Tokyo). Upon graduation, he returned to Naha where he would later become director of the Okinawa Prefectural Library. In addition to his work at the library, Ifa devoted himself to shedding light on every aspect of Okinawan history and culture. Eventually, he left behind his wife and family and eloped to Tokyo with a young woman. There, he became impoverished and struggled to continue his Okinawan studies. Soon after the end of the war in 1947, he drew his last breath, still worrying about the fate

---

1. He wrote his name with this spelling in English, reflecting the Okinawan pronunciation, even though the strict Japanese romanization would be Iha Fuyū.

of his beloved Okinawa. Back in his hometown, his family had lost everything, leaving him without a place to be laid to rest. A group of his devoted pupils hastened to select a gravesite on the grounds of the Urasoe Castle Ruins and brought his remains to Okinawa for burial.

The tomb, set against massive blocks of Ryukyuan limestone, is in a green park, surrounded by trees. A monument in a nearby corner is engraved with a few lines by Ifa's friend and fellow scholar Higashionna Kanjun:

> Father of Okinawan and *Omoro* studies[2]
> None knew more about Okinawa
> None loved Okinawa better
> None grieved more for Okinawa
> He loved because he understood, and he grieved because he loved
> He was a scholar, a patriot, and a prophet.

Early Studies in Japanese Linguistics

When Ifa was studying at the Third Higher School, he wrote a short essay in the local newspaper expressing his determination to become a pioneering scholar of Ryukyuan history, but by the time he entered Tokyo Imperial University, he seems to have changed his mind, switching from history to linguistics. Ifa was a member of the inaugural class in the Department of Linguistics, along with Hashimoto Shinkichi (Japanese linguistics) also from the Third Higher School, and Ogura Shinpei (Korean linguistics); Kindaichi Kyōsuke (Ainu linguistics) followed in the department's second cohort. Along with Ifa

---

2. *Omoro* studies is the study of the *Omoro sōshi*, a compilation of Ryukyuan poems, songs, and oracles.

CHAPTER I

Fuyū (Ryukyuan linguistics), this group went on to lay the foundations for the linguistic study of Japanese and its neighboring languages.

They studied under Professor Ueda Kazutoshi and Assistant Professor Niimura Izuru; Ueda had been a student of the British academic and Japanologist Basil Hall Chamberlain, who introduced the methodologies of linguistics to Japan. In 1816, Chamberlain's maternal grandfather, Captain Basil Hall, had visited the Ryukyu Kingdom and introduced it to the West two years later in his *Account of a Voyage of Discovery*.[3] Chamberlain himself wrote a long treatise on the Ryukyuan language when he was resident in Japan. Ifa's study on Ryukyuan linguistics began during the formative years of the Department of Linguistics at Tokyo Imperial University, and built directly on the results of Basil Hall Chamberlain's research. Armed with linguistics, he began to explore the unknown wilds of Okinawa's history and culture.

In his later years, Ifa would say he did not need a funeral or a tomb. Instead of a funeral, he said, he would prefer that a panel discussion be held. If he had to have a grave, he hoped to rest in the memories of the people of his homeland.

Ifa Fuyū (1876–1947). Reproduced from Ifa Fuyū, *Ryūkyū seiten omoshirosaushi sen: Omoro ni arawaretaru ko Ryūkyū no bunka* (Ishizuka Shoten, 1924). NDL Digital Collections.

---

3. Basil Hall, *Account of a Voyage of Discovery to the West Coast of Corea and the Great Loo-Choo Island* (London: John Murray, 1818).

"Existing without knowing oneself is miserable," he said. "My friends and I don't explain things to each other by arguing or singing songs. We explain ourselves with our own existence." This was his stance regarding Okinawa, and it resonates deeply with me.

So, what was behind Ifa's struggle to establish a field of Okinawan studies? In modern history, the aftermath of Kawakami Hajime's infamous Careless Words Incident would become deeply intertwined with this struggle.

2. Kawakami Hajime's Careless Words

Kawakami Hajime Visits Okinawa

Assistant Professor Kawakami Hajime of Kyoto Imperial University first stepped foot on the island of Okinawa when he disembarked from the vessel *Bazan Maru* on April 1, 1911. Perhaps he started his two-week research trip to Okinawa by changing out of his travel clothes at the Ikehata Ryokan where he was staying and pondering about the days to come. An article welcoming Kawakami was published in the local *Okinawa Mainichi Shimbun* that day.

Kawakami then walked about fifteen minutes to the Okinawa Prefectural Library where he met and politely greeted Director Ifa Fuyū for the first time. In the reading room, he immediately opened his notebook and started taking notes on materials related to the system of land allocation. At this time, Kawakami was thirty-three years old, to Ifa Fuyū's thirty-six.

Two days later on April 3, at the request of the Okinawa Prefectural Board of Education, Kawakami delivered a ninety-minute lecture entitled "A New Age Is Coming" to an audience of five hundred gathered at Naha's Matsuyama Elementary School. The audience would have included members of the former ruling class of Shuri, as well as bureaucrats and merchants from the mainland, all figures who played leading roles in Okinawan society. After the lecture, a welcome party was held from 6 p.m. with fifty to sixty guests in attendance. It is thought that many of Okinawa's foremost experts made an appearance that night. The party took place at the banquet hall known as Fūgetsurō (Tower of the Wind and Moon). This hall was built on an exposed reef in Naha Port, atop the ancient foundations of the royal storehouse from the brilliant, long-past days of overseas envoy missions to China. Fūgetsurō was Okinawa's most luxurious restaurant, with geisha from the mainland waiting upon the banquets. There are no known records of the mood at the reception, but considering the situation that played out immediately afterwards, it was certainly an awkward time for many of those involved.

The next morning, on the fourth, Kawakami was back at the Prefectural Library. He returned to copying excerpts from materials related to the land system, as well as from the manuscript of *Ko Ryūkyū* (Ancient Ryukyu), Ifa's first full-fledged publication. That evening, Kawakami attended a lecture by Ifa on the subject of Okinawan religion.

On the fifth, Ifa accompanied Kawakami to Itoman, a fishing village in the south of Okinawa Island, to conduct some research. In the evening, their survey completed, they returned to their lodgings, where Kawakami was no doubt shocked to find himself in the *Ryukyu Shinpo*. The newspaper had published an account of his lecture, "A New Age Is Coming," but it also contained a critical editorial titled, "A Traveler's Critique of the Prefecture." This editorial was the first of a barrage of criticism aimed at Kawakami from the local newspapers (especially the *Ryukyu Shinpo*), starting what would later become known as the Careless Words Incident.

It is unclear what Kawakami did on the sixth, but on the seventh, he appears to have made a research visit to the village of Nakagusuku at the center of Okinawa Island. Then, on the eighth, he gave a lecture entitled "Contradiction and Harmony" to thirty sympathetic young attendees at Meirindō in Kume. He then departed from Okinawa on the Kagoshima-bound *Okinawa Maru* to escape the hostile atmosphere that had formed around him. His planned two-week visit to research the land system had been cut in half.

The Ideology of Loyalty and Patriotism

We might wonder what passages in "A New Age Is Coming" lay at the root of this incident. After speaking at length on new ideas, Kawakami made the following comment referring specifically to Okinawa:

> Upon observation, it is clear that the history of Okinawa's language, traditions, customs, and beliefs and ideas differ in every aspect from that of the mainland. Some might even say the people of Okinawa scarcely hold to the ideology of loyalty and patriotism. However, these are not things to be regretted. Even with all this, I have the highest expectations of Okinawa, and I am deeply interested in it as well.... Now, as a part of Japan, where we are fervent and unified in our love of country, a region like this, somewhat weaker in its patriotic fervor, is most interesting to me. History gives us examples of great leaders who dominated an era but were born into nations with weak national bonds. For example, the Judea of Christ's time, or Śakyamuni's India. Shattered countries produced some great leaders in antiquity. Had Judea or India not been in crisis, these great men would not have been born. Thus, even if this prefecture is weakened by its lack of loyalty and patriotism, with the needs of a new age, I truly anticipate that a new hero will someday rise from among you, and I feel a deep interest in this.

In short, Kawakami stressed that in contrast to Japanese society with its strong sense of loyalty, patriotism, and national fervor, Okinawa's potential lay in its relative difference, and its circumstances would produce new leaders for the future. In this, Kawakami may simply have been too far ahead of his time. Today, over eighty years later, there is widespread acceptance of the idea that Okinawa's uniqueness is also its potential. However, the leaders of Okinawan society at the time felt quite differently, and their resulting criticism of Kawakami can only be described as extreme.

The local newspapers accused Kawakami of being an "anti-patriotic instigator," and criticized his statement that Okinawans lacked "sincere loyalty and patriotism" as the height of disrespect. Comparing Okinawa to such "shattered countries" as Judea and India was the same as spitting in the face of the Okinawan people and the papers condemned Kawakami's speech as "words that could not be unheard." From the perspective of Okinawa's leaders, actively engaged in dispelling local discomfort with Yamato (mainland Japan) in order to promote Okinawa's integration into Imperial Japan, Kawakami's words were unforgivable. Pursued by this firestorm of criticism and slander, Kawakami fled Okinawa.

Soon after returning to Kyoto in 1911, Kawakami published an essay, "Ryūkyū Itoman no kojin shugi teki kazoku" (Individualist Families in Ryukyu Itoman), which included the following paragraph:

> When I visited Ryukyu, I was invited to give a lecture. I concluded with some examples of the special characteristics I hoped to see in the Ryukyuan people, but some of the gentlemen in the audience misunderstood me. This led to distortions, which were followed by attacks, and finally outright insults, until suddenly, a new phenomenon had appeared in the land of Ryukyu!

There is so much to investigate and consider there. These solitary islands in the far southern reaches of the empire have a long and unique history set in a special landscape, very unlike the rivers and mountains of our own homeland. The profound differences extend to the culture, economic and government systems, customs, and ideologies held by these people. If anyone were to insult this extraordinary singularity of Okinawa, I would not hesitate to condemn them.[4]

In a postscript to Ifa Fuyū's book *Ko Ryūkyū* (Ancient Ryukyu) published late the same year, Kawakami wrote, "In retrospect, I visited there once, and gave a lecture. Unexpectedly, I received a barrage of criticism from the many intellectuals there. It was almost too much to bear. I have already been brought down by my words, though I still have some thoughts on the matter. However, if my writings were to invite further criticism, I would no longer be able to bear it."

When I read these lines, Kawakami's regret over the misunderstanding of his intended meaning, being called "anti-patriotic," and feeling forced to leave Okinawa immediately, seems clear. At the same time, his claim that his position on Okinawa remained the same resonates with me.

In the past I spent some time in the Kawakami Hajime collection of Kyoto University's Faculty of Economics, reading and making copies of the three research notebooks he filled while he was in Okinawa. Kawakami's strong interest in learning more about Okinawa comes through clearly in his beautiful, calligraphic writing. Though he was able to stay for only a week, his notes are stuffed with excerpts from relevant documents and memoirs. I felt my own sense of regret that his research had been cut off prematurely due to his careless words.

---

4. Kawakami Hajime, "Ryūkyū Itoman no kojin shugi teki kazoku" [Individualist Families in Ryukyu Itoman], *Kyoto Imperial University Law Association Journal* 6–9 (1911): 111–114.

CHAPTER I

"Like-minded" Ifa Fuyū

The issue Kawakami presented was important. Okinawa is indeed unique in many ways, and the problem wasn't that he pointed this out; many scholars both before and since have made the same point. The important point here is that he highlighted Okinawa's distinctiveness in relation to the state of contemporary Japanese society, recognizing Okinawa's unique characteristics and using them to critique Japan's national ideologies. In other words, he held that the Japanese state was unable to properly value Okinawa's differences, and thus was not properly contemplating how to make use of Okinawa within the national framework. The novel element of his talk was his criticism of how Japan followed the ideology of loyalty and patriotism so fervently.

The swirl of controversy around Kawakami's comments may have prevented him from continuing his research, but Ifa Fuyū's complete absence from the storm must be noted. Though he supported Kawakami's research by providing materials, accompanying him on research trips, and delivering private lectures, there is no evidence that Ifa openly defended him. At best, he prompted his younger brother, Ifa Getsujō, a reporter at the *Okinawa Mainichi Shimbun*, to run a campaign defending Kawakami.

However, in his inimitable, unobtrusive style, Ifa was certainly sympathetic to Kawakami's ideas. We know this because despite the outrage Kawakami had provoked earlier the same year, Ifa made a point of including a postscript by Kawakami, as mentioned earlier, in his monumental work *Ko Ryūkyū*, regarded by most Okinawans as having launched the field of Ryukyuan studies. Also, after he had fled back to Kyoto following the Careless Words Incident, Kawakami sent Ifa a copy of his essay titled "Thoughts on How Emperor Sujin's Reorganization of the Jingu Imperial Palace Represented an Important Period of National Unification," which Ifa drew on for his book *Ko*

Ryūkyū no seiji (The Politics of Ancient Ryukyu, 1922), published eleven years after the incident. "I was surprised to see this essay was written in the same style as my work on the reign of King Shō Shin," Ifa wrote. He included Kawakami's arguments in detail, using them to make his own points. Finally, on the title page he outright dedicated *Ko Ryūkyū no seiji* to Kawakami: "This little book is dedicated to Doctor Kawakami Hajime, whom I respect."

There is more. In his later years, Kawakami joined the Communist Party and threw himself into political activities. He was arrested and placed under house arrest in 1943. Hearing of this, Ifa, who was living in Tokyo at the time, frequently sent gifts such as books he had authored and Okinawan candy made from raw sugar, and wrote letters to help Kawakami keep his spirits up. In the last days of that year, on December 28, Ifa stopped on a trip to Osaka to visit Kawakami. In his journal entry for that day, Kawakami wrote, "Mr. Ifa Fuyū paid me a visit a little after 3 o'clock. Even though it has been thirty-plus years since we met, yesterday he was just as I remembered, and we spent a pleasant time chatting like old friends. Of all recent events, I think this one made me happiest. At 5 o'clock, I walked him to Higashi Ichijō train station." The next day he added, "Getting to meet Mr. Ifa yesterday left me so happy that I was still feeling elated after dinner, and my excitement has not waned in the slightest."[5]

Ifa respected Kawakami, and found in him a comrade, a kindred spirit, whose ideas resonated with his own. In the maelstrom that swirled around the Careless Words Incident, Ifa did not abandon Kawakami. Though he may have appeared slow to do so, Ifa's support was made clear through his persistent efforts.

---

5. Kawakami Hajime, *Ban'nen no seikatsu kiroku ge* [Record of My Final Years, Vol. 2] (Tokyo: Daiichi Shorin, 1958): 93. National Diet Library Digital Collections. https://dl.ndl.go.jp/pid/2972744. Accessed April 19, 2024.

CHAPTER I

3. The Origin of Uniqueness

Ifa Fuyū's Struggle

In fact, Ifa held similar views with Kawakami before they even met. In 1907, four years before Kawakami came to Okinawa, Ifa had delivered a lecture at the request of the same group that sponsored Kawakami's talk, the Okinawa Prefectural Education Association, at a program held at the Okinawa Prefectural Normal School. After his talk, titled "Views on How to Approach Local History," in which he addressed the Okinawan people's history of hardship and suffering, Ifa added a message to the gathered "experts" (former Shuri court officials, bureaucrats from the mainland, businessmen from outside the prefecture, and so on):

> I believe that it is possible for Okinawa to be a part of the powerful Japanese Empire because there are many undeniable points of similarity between us. But, if we allow the successive destruction, through sheer inertia, of the characteristics unique to Ryukyu, it will break the spiritual connection between the two peoples [Japanese and Okinawan]. That is ignoring history. So, as I said, it is important to show our points of similarity, but it is even more important to recognize our differences. To be sure, calling them mere "differences" is somewhat misleading, but let's define these as the characteristics that no other can imitate. I believe every individual has unique characteristics that cannot be imitated by others.[6]

Ifa stressed that in addition to showcasing Okinawa's similarities with

---

6. Published in *Okinawa Shimbun*, date unknown.

mainland Japan, acknowledging their differences was also important. Choosing his words carefully, he advocated for an end to "the tendency to disregard the unique aspects of Ryukyu" and to break away from the folly of "ignoring history," urging his audience to give up their prejudicial biases.

So why didn't Ifa openly take a stand in Kawakami's defense during the incident? It is my theory that for Kawakami, this event was only momentary. When the situation became untenable, he escaped easily by departing the scene. However, for Ifa, the event took place on his home territory, where he must continue to lead his daily life. There was no running away without dire consequences. Faced with a social situation full of pitfalls, he concealed his determination to somehow overcome it and chose a path of discretion in order to preserve his career as a scholar of Okinawa. For Ifa, the incident was just a minor local conflict. I think that from Ifa's standpoint, as he continued to struggle to understand the much larger front of Okinawan issues as a whole, the matter was simply not worth the fight that would ensue.

How might Okinawa, with its special cultural characteristics, fit within Japanese society? Kawakami's argument linked the answer to this question directly to the nature of Japanese society. Ifa, on the other hand, while agreeing in principle with Kawakami, had to engage in the tortured logic of acknowledging Okinawa's similarities, but also its points of difference, all while highlighting its special qualities.

Perhaps when Okinawans tried to hold up their own unique, treasured culture as the basis for taking issue with Japanese society, they came to understand that Japanese society was unyielding in its ideology of "loyalty and patriotism," and that in a culture which so highly valued uniformity, difference would not be tolerated.

CHAPTER I

Issues Left Unanswered

As I read about the Kawakami incident, I thought again about Okinawa's uniqueness. Just how has the field of Okinawan studies since then handled the issues about which Kawakami spoke so directly, and about which Ifa hemmed and hawed?

This may serve as a rather coarse generalization, but the field has largely ignored the issue. Modern Japan has tended toward a more demanding ideology that compels uniformity rather than fostering diversity. Thus, for Okinawans, it has been a process of being forced to demonstrate points of similarity. Moreover, the overall tone of Okinawan studies has helped contribute to this trend.

With the participation of Yanagita Kunio, Orikuchi Shinobu, and others, Okinawan studies came to focus on folklore and ethnology. In the case of Okinawa, many customs and traditions have been preserved that could shed significant light on our understanding of ancient Japan and seeking out these shared historical commonalities became popular. As if in response to this trend, Okinawa began to produce native teachers and researchers who authored a great number of reports on folk customs. This flood of research, in fact, deserves special mention for the ties it created between Okinawan and mainland Japanese researchers, and for laying the foundation of Okinawan folk culture theory. However, when it came to the issue Kawakami advocated, and which Ifa avoided, this new research stayed away from the most important points in question.

While Okinawa's distinctive folk customs were being collected and tabulated, the historical context in which they developed was kept firmly in the background. Nor was there, in these copious scholarly reports, any discussion of how Japanese society should be composed, including the incorporation of Okinawa with its unique culture.

Then came the Battle of Okinawa and the postwar era under US occupation. The return-to-the-fatherland movement that developed under this foreign regime began with demands for the restoration of basic human rights, anti-war peace protests, and more, as Okinawans' political awareness soared and they sought to return to their place in the Japanese constitutional system.

The field of historical research, paralleling this political awakening, began to center on modern topics like the annexation of Ryukyu in 1879. Scholars explored questions about the Ryukyu issue in the context of ethnic integration and unification in Japan. Additionally, discussion arose about the nature of post-annexation modern Okinawa, with the aim of understanding how to perceive the characteristics of modern Japan. With this, we can say scholars were finally giving serious consideration to the issues that Kawakami addressed so forthrightly.

At the same time, in my opinion, the new focus on the Disposition of Ryukyu and its aftereffects lacked a thorough examination and understanding of the unique qualities of the newly created Okinawa Prefecture. In other words, there was no clear, overarching vision for Okinawa's premodern history, that is, of the Ryukyu Kingdom, the very premise for Okinawa's modern history.

What exactly is the true nature of Okinawa's uniqueness? What characteristics unique to the region influenced events as Okinawa moved toward unification and colored its integration with modern Japan post-annexation? These questions have seen far too little discussion.

This is how I interpret what Kawakami Hajime said clearly out loud, and what Ifa Fuyū wanted to say but could not: Okinawa was once an independent nation known as the Ryukyu Kingdom, having developed unique features during its long stretch of history outside the Japanese polity. When the kingdom was abolished, a new era for Okinawa began inside the borders of Japan. However, the problem remains that this new Okinawa still contains within itself many of those special features developed during its period of independence as the Ryukyu Kingdom. This is why Kawakami perceived a weak sense of national spirit and why, from the Okinawan perspective, "Yamato" refers to mainland Japan and does not include Okinawa, and Okinawa still preserves its unique traits to remain distinct from the rest of Japan.

Okinawa gave rise to a kingdom that came into existence outside of Japan's national system, but over time, the kingdom underwent a historical process of integration into Japanese society. As a result, the objective in the field of premodern Okinawan history is to elucidate the formation process, substance, and subsequent transformations of this kingdom, while the objective in modern Okinawan history is to show how the kingdom collapsed and how its territory was reorganized as a part of Japanese society.

The historical view informed by the single-nation theory, which holds that Japan has evolved since the dawn of history as a single, monolithic culture, suppressed Kawakami's argument and fractured Ifa's. If this is the case, we can only access the legacy of our ancestors if we start by painting a portrait of the Ryukyu Kingdom that shatters this myth of a single national origin. Thus, the main theme of my research into premodern history is to present the Ryukyu Kingdom as another nation that existed within the bounds of Japanese society.

CHAPTER II
ANCIENT RYUKYU

CHAPTER II

1. The Period of Transformation Begins

The Dawn of Okinawan History

The islands of Okinawa show evidence of human habitation from as early as the Paleolithic era.[1] Among the most important finds for physical anthropologists in search of the roots of the Japanese people, Minatogawa Man, carbon-dated to about 18,000 years ago, was discovered in the southern part of the main island of Okinawa.[2] The Jōmon period began in mainland Japan between 10,000 to 13,000 years ago, and a type of Jōmon pottery known as *tsumegatamon* (fingernail impression pattern) pottery has been found in various locations around Okinawa, confirming that Jōmon culture entered the islands from an early period. The people who lived in and formed the first communities in the islands were a part of the cultural sphere based in the islands of prehistoric Japan. If one can be forgiven for using the term "proto-Japanese culture," then it can be said that the people of the Okinawan islands and mainland Japan shared a common culture from the earliest times.

Even so, in the late Jōmon period, Okinawan pottery culture became more distinctive, with cultural styles associated with the prehistoric Japanese mainland gradually fading away. In the following Yayoi period, excavations in Okinawa have unearthed plenty of pottery that

---

1. The Japanese Paleolithic period spans from 35,000 BCE to about 13,000 BCE.
2. An even older find, Yamashita Cave Man, discovered in Naha City, has been dated to as early as 32,000 years ago.

resembles Yayoi pottery, but most archaeologists are not convinced that this was accompanied by the rice cultivation that formed the basis of Yayoi culture. Within the limits of present-day archaeological evidence, we can observe that the influence of Yayoi culture on Okinawa was strikingly limited compared to that on Yamato society on the mainland. After the Yayoi period, Yamato society experienced rapid and profound changes as it transitioned from the Kofun period to the Asuka and Nara periods which saw the adoption of a legal system of national government modeled after the philosophies of Confucianism and Chinese legalism (*ritsuryō*). In contrast, people in Okinawa were still living in coastal lowlands gathering shellfish and catching fish in shallow lagoons hemmed in by coral reefs. They likely spent peaceful, sleepy days there in the southern islands.

That is not to say Okinawa was isolated from the outside world at that time. The East China Sea functioned like an inland sea, permitting regular exchanges between the communities around its periphery. In Kyushu, a Yayoi-period tomb yielded an arm bone wearing a bangle made from a conch shell believed to have come from Okinawan waters. Chinese coins minted in periods from the Warring States period (403–221 BCE) through to the Tang dynasty (618–907 CE) have also been excavated from many archaeological sites in Okinawa, including knife coins, Wu Zhu cash coins, and Kaiyuan Tongbao cash coins.

Furthermore, texts such as the *Nihon shoki* (The Chronicles of Japan) and *Shoku Nihongi* (The Chronicles of Japan Continued) record that the people in the islands south of Kyushu, including a part of Okinawa (collectively called the "Southern Islands"), sent tribute to Yamato and were bestowed rank around the seventh and eighth centuries. When sailing along the coast of the Korean Peninsula became dangerous, Japanese mission ships bound for Tang China began island-hopping via the sea route south of Kyushu, and the Yamato state was actively involved in securing that passage. In 753 CE, a ship carrying the famous monk Jianzhen (J. Ganjin) drifted ashore to "Akonapa Island," commonly accepted to have been present-day Okinawa Island, where he stayed for a short time before continuing his journey to Yamato.[3]

Incidentally, the *Sui shu* (Book of Sui, 636 CE), an official history of the Chinese Sui dynasty, contains a tantalizing entry. This is a fairly detailed description of the customs and traditions of a country on the edge of the East China Sea, identified as "Ryukyu" and written as 流求[4] (Ch. *Liuqiu*), a land outside the Sinosphere (i.e., a backward region not under China's civilizing influence). Some of the descriptions seem to resemble Okinawa, but the text also includes information on flora and fauna not found there, making the document difficult to decipher. Since before World War II, there have been conflicting theories that this "Ryukyu" referred to Taiwan while others believed it meant Okinawa. And yet another theory posits that the written descriptions of Taiwan and Okinawa have been mixed up. Even now, no convincing interpretation has been presented to explain the matter.

Thus, the evidence certainly confirms that there were exchanges with various overseas regions. However, these exchanges were not constant, and the physical and written traces we have do not indicate the kind of continuous contact that would have completely changed the lifestyles of the people living on Okinawa's islands. Yamato's involvement in the "Southern Islands" was not stable, and Okinawa does not seem to have been the final destination for ships loaded with Chinese goods. In the end, we must conclude that the people of these islands led fairly quiet lives fishing and collecting shellfish in their lagoons. Archaeologists refer to this period of gathering culture that

---

3. Wang Xiangrong, ed., *Tang dahe shangdong zhengchuan* [True Account of the China-Yamato Eastern Expedition] (Beijing: Zhonghua Shuju, 2000).
4. cf. Today, Ryukyu is usually written with the Chinese characters 琉球.

continued for centuries after the end of the Jōmon period as the Shell Mound period.

One notable fact in all this is that even though the island groups of Miyako and Yaeyama (known collectively as Sakishima), are now included when we talk about Okinawa, no Jōmon- or Yayoi-era pottery has ever been found there. In contrast, the influence of Southeast Asia and the South Pacific is evident in the earthenware pots featuring earlike protrusions (*gaiji doki*); hatchets made from the shells of giant clams; and stones used for stone boiling cooking, that have been unearthed in digs there. There was no single, unified culture within Okinawa, but a richness of variation spread throughout.

However, as has been made clear through long years of linguistics research, the dialects spoken in Miyako and Yaeyama, along with those of Amami and Okinawa, together constitute the Ryukyuan dialect that is a part of the Japonic language family.[5] That said, why does the material culture of Sakishima have a "South Seas" flavor to it? This is at the heart of a rather mysterious puzzle.

Beginning of the Gusuku Period

Starting around the twelfth century, the peaceful life of the islands abruptly took on a busier rhythm, ushering in innovations during a time archaeologists have dubbed the Gusuku period. This period had the following characteristics.

First, great quantities of carbonized rice and wheat have been found in Gusuku-era excavations, establishing that Okinawa had become an agrarian society with grain cultivation. Second, from the

---

5. The Ryukyuan language and all its dialects constitute a sister language to Japanese. Together, they form the Japonic family of languages, with Proto-Japonic as their mother language.

many iron utensils that have been found, especially swords (knife-like cutting tools), ironworking had clearly begun in earnest. Third, *sue* stoneware[6] from the island of Tokunoshima in the Amami group was being traded throughout the islands, reflecting movement toward an increasingly unified cultural sphere in the area. Places of worship, fortresses, and other structures, known as *gusuku, gushiku,* or *suku,* also made their appearance during this period. Fourth, dig finds including Chinese ceramics and talcum stone cooking pots (J. *kasseki-sei ishinabe*) from mainland Japan indicate that foreign cultures exerted continuous influence. Fifth, in addition to now living mainly on the limestone plateaus and hilly areas, people began to use natural spring water to cultivate small-scale rice paddies, which was a major change from the land-use patterns of the past. Finally, sixth, in response to these social changes, a chieftain class known as *aji* (O. *anji*), emerged and formed small, local governing entities. They built strongholds known as *gusuku* and vied with each other as the times grew increasingly turbulent.

Why did this era of change come to Okinawa? This question cannot be answered solely by looking at conditions within the islands. This is because the beginning of the Gusuku period was marked by comprehensive and structural factors symbolized by the impact of foreign culture. We must look at trends in the international communities surrounding Okinawa to understand local changes.

The first example that comes to mind is the energy that was overflowing from the Japanese mainland as an ancient society transitioned to a medieval one centered on the newly emergent and powerful samurai clans. Then there were the *wakō,* or *kaikō,*

---

6. These are now known as Kamuiyaki ware, named after the place where the kilns were discovered on Tokunoshima.

Figure 1. **Comparative Timeline for the Historic Periods of Ryukyu/Okinawa and Japan**

Ryukyu - Okinawa			Japan	
Prehistoric period	Paleolithic period	8,000 BCE	Paleolithic period	
	Shell Mound period Neolithic period	5,000 BCE	Jōmon period	
			Yayoi period	
			Ancient period (Kofun, Asuka, Nara, and Heian eras)	
Ancient Ryukyu	Gusuku period	12th c.	Kamakura period	Medieval period
	Sanzan	14th c.	Northern and Southern Courts period	
	First Shō dynasty	15th c.	Muromachi period	
	Second Shō dynasty (early)	1470	Warring States period	
		Shimazu Invasion, 1609	Azuchi-Momoyama period	Early modern period
Early modern Ryukyu	Second Shō dynasty (later)		Edo (Tokugawa) period	
			Modern era	
Modern Okinawa	Okinawa Prefecture	Disposition of Ryukyu, 1879		
		Battle of Okinawa, 1945		
Postwar Okinawa	Return to Japanese Rule, 1972	US Governance period	Current era	
	Okinawa Prefecture			

CHAPTER II

armed private traders (essentially pirates) who likely frequented the Okinawan islands. Another probable source of change was the influx of people with skills in agriculture and blacksmithing who introduced more advanced techniques. No historical materials or documents have been found that shed light on the details of this story, but the dramatic changes of the Gusuku period are difficult to explain unless we assume a steady and continuous flow of people, goods, and information. This is a subject I hope future Japanese historical research will devote attention to.

Another point concerns events in mainland China. When the northern Jin people conquered northern China, the Song dynasty retreated south to Jiangnan and reorganized to form the Southern Song dynasty. This invigorated southern China which underwent rapid development and experienced a flourishing of maritime trade. Artifacts from this period, including older Chinese ceramics like white porcelain from the Southern Song era, unearthed from Okinawan dig sites suggest that the impact of changes in mainland China on Okinawa should not be overlooked.

At any rate, around the twelfth century, maritime traffic on the East China Sea became more active than ever before. The change and upheaval that affected the Okinawan lifestyle most likely came from the changes accompanying the rise of the samurai clans in Japan, and the power the Southern Song dynasty exerted in trade. To be clear, this was in no way a case of numerous outsiders invading or seizing control of the Okinawan islands; rather, I wish to emphasize that the profound changes witnessed in the islands unfolded rapidly with the flood of people, goods, and information from the areas around the East China Sea.

2. The Road to the Kingdom

Three Spheres of Influence Emerge

The vitality of the Gusuku period set the stage for the formation of the Ryukyu Kingdom. The conflicts that had flared between the local *aji* who had consolidated power to become leaders in their respective areas eventually led to the founding of the kingdom.

In the fourteenth century, three spheres of influence coalesced around the most powerful *aji* on the main island of Okinawa. In the island's northern region, the Nakijin *aji*, ruled over the "northern mountain" of Sanhoku from his base at Nakijin Castle. The Urasoe *aji* reigned in the "central mountain" of Chūzan, based at Urasoe Castle in the central part of the island. And the Ōzato *aji*, based at Shimajiri Ōzato Castle or Shimazoe Ōzato depending on the time period, was supreme leader in the southern area known as Sannan, i.e., the "southern mountain." These three *aji*, all styling themselves as "kings," formed the three corners of the triangular balance of power during the Sanzan (three mountains) period. Even today, there is a custom of dividing Okinawa's main island into three parts that dates back to the Sanzan period: the "head of the country" Kunigami in the north, the central "head of the middle" Nakagami, and the southern "island tail" Shimajiri.

However, even though they called themselves "kings," their rank was in reality no more than leader of a loose collection of *aji*, all joined in an alliance to extend power over an area with a *gusuku* or fortress at its center. In fact, internal fights over who should be the top leader were common in Sannan and often concluded with a newcomer claiming the title of "King of Sannan."

Eventually, the tension and antagonism between the three kingdoms would have most likely ended with the consolidation of a unified power, but this process was accelerated by outside forces. This force

CHAPTER II

Figure 2. *Gusuku* of the Sanzan Era

Gusuku, also known as *gushiku* or *suku*, now generally refers to a fortress located on a slight elevation. However, many of these *gusuku* have no fortress-like structures at all, leading to competing but unconfirmed theories that these may have been sacred precincts, or that they are simply the remains of ancient settlements. There are believed to be more than two hundred *gusuku* sites throughout Okinawa, but aside from a few exceptions, no excavation surveys have been conducted. Notable examples of *gusuku* with remaining stonework include the fortifications at Nakijin Castle and Nakagusuku.

did not come from Japan in the north, but from China in the west, across the East China Sea.

The Mongolian Yuan dynasty, which had long ruled China, finally fell in 1368, and the Ming dynasty was founded by ethnic Han Chinese. Shock waves from this dramatic power shift swiftly reached the Okinawan islands. Hongwu, the first emperor of the Ming dynasty, immediately sent emissaries to surrounding nations to announce the new dynasty and to demand fealty. Four years later, in 1372, a mission was dispatched to Ryukyu, headed by imperial envoy Yang Zai who urged King Satto of Sanzan's Chūzan domain to pay tribute.

Payment of tribute was a diplomatic act of submission to express allegiance to Chinese imperial power. The imperial edict that Yang Zai brought decreed that China would now be called "Great Ming," and the current era name was "Hongwu." It noted that when emissaries had been sent to the surrounding lands, many of those countries had paid tribute, adding, "Since Ryukyu lies far across the ocean to China's southeast, there are still those who know nothing of its existence. Accordingly, a special envoy has been dispatched to explain the matter clearly." In fact, this entry in the *Ming shi lu* (Annals of the Ming Dynasty) represents the earliest recorded use of the name "Ryukyu" written as 琉球 (Ch. *Liuqiu*). From then on, the Amami, Okinawa, and Sakishima island groups also fell under the name of "Ryukyu." Thus, before Sanzan could even extend its control over the other islands and name them, "Ryukyu" was imposed on all of them by outsiders.

Yang Zai's visit to Ryukyu had a powerful impact on its subsequent history. The Ryukyuan side could have turned down the Ming invitation, but considering its internal situation of conflict between the Sanzan domains, it must have seemed like an unexpected windfall. Besides the huge profits to be made off the so-called tribute missions, the legitimacy this would bestow on Ryukyu's rulers was irresistible.

CHAPTER II

The relationship with the Ming dynasty's global empire that Yang Zai's visit offered to Chūzan's King Satto would place him in a position of great advantage over his rivals in Sanhoku and Sannan. As a note of interest, this entry in the Ming annals, which records King Satto's name, makes him the first-ever confirmed and named figure in Ryukyuan history.

So, what exactly was the purpose behind Yang Zai's visit to such a remote island, urging its leaders to pay tribute? He actually had two reasons. The first, obviously, was to add Ryukyu to the network of nations that formed the world order with the Chinese emperor at its zenith.[7] Secondly, and perhaps more urgently, he wanted horses[8] and sulfur. Although the Mongol forces had been driven beyond the Great Wall, they were looking for opportunities to return, and the Ming dynasty had to mount continuous military operations against them. For this, the Ming needed sulfur to make gunpowder and horses for transporting military supplies and munitions to the front lines.

In order to declare his intention of joining the system of tributary nations, King Satto appointed his younger brother, Taiki, as the head of a diplomatic mission to accompany Yang Zai back to China. Taiki thus became the first Ryukyuan to cross the East China Sea on official business. From that year onwards, the Chūzan king dispatched ships to China every year, and as a result, it looked as though he had the power to dominate his rival domains.

However, this does not mean that Sanhoku and Sannan just quietly ignored Chūzan's actions. In 1380, eight years after Taiki crossed the East China Sea for the first time, the king of Sannan, Shō Satto, also sent an envoy to China and joined Chūzan as a member of China's tributary nations. Then, three years later in 1383, King Hanishi of

---

7. The system of tributary nations or the suzerain-vassal system (J. *sakuhō taisei / sappō taisei*).
8. Okinawa is home to several small, indigenous horse breeds.

Sanhoku did the same. The resulting predicament was the single entity of Ryukyu being represented by three different rulers, each with diplomatic ties to China. The plans of King Satto of Chūzan had been easily foiled, and the three domains found themselves back where they had started.

Against this backdrop of involvement with China, the focus of our history narrows down to one question: Who finally achieved the dream of Ryukyuan unification? Surprisingly, it was not any of the self-styled "kings" of Chūzan, Sannan, or Sanhoku. Instead, there was a dark horse waiting for his opportunity.

Establishment of a Unified Dynasty

The Sashiki *aji*, Shishō, was just a minor local chief under the king of Sannan, based at Sashiki-Ui Gusuku. However, his son Shō Hashi, appears to have been of exceptional talent. In 1406, father and son joined forces to attack Urasoe Castle. They overthrew Satto's successor Bunei, and Shishō became king. According to the *Annals of the Ming Dynasty*, Shishō sent an envoy representing him as the "crown prince" (heir) of the Ryukyu Chūzan King Bunei, to announce the death of his "father" and request official imperial recognition. Because usurpation by force could have invited negative consequences, Shishō engaged in this pretense of being the "heir" succeeding to his "father's" throne. In response, the Ming emperor Yongle sent an investiture mission the following year to formally invest Shishō as king of Chūzan. Immediately after this elaborate exchange, Shō Hashi moved the capital of Chūzan from Urasoe to Shuri Castle (Shuri Gusuku) and began to transform the old fortress there into a citadel worthy of Chūzan's new king. This was the start of the First Shō dynasty, which would subsequently establish the Ryukyu Kingdom.

CHAPTER II

Nakijin Gusuku (top) served as the base for Sanhoku. Katsuren Gusuku (bottom) is famous as Amawari's stronghold (see page 57). Photos by Takara Kurayoshi.

In 1416, Shō Hashi dispatched a large army to attack Nakijin Castle and defeated Sanhoku's King Han'anchi. Sanhoku's territory was absorbed into Chūzan, and the names of Sanhoku kings ceased to appear in the *Annals of the Ming Dynasty*. When Shishō died in 1421, Shō Hashi succeeded him to become the second king of the First Shō dynasty, and his new status was formalized in 1425 by Chai Shan, the investiture envoy sent by Emperor Yongle. Finally, in 1427, Shuri Castle's outer gardens underwent extensive improvements and saw the addition of an artificial pond named Ryūtan (lit. "dragon pool"), all under the supervision of Huai Ji, a Chinese political advisor serving Shō Hashi. These projects were meant to showcase the growth and success of Chūzan, now even more powerful after its annexation of Sanhoku.[9]

Now only Sannan remained. Chūzan forces assaulted Sannan in 1429, seizing Shimajiri Ōsato Gusuku and ending King Taromii's reign. Now, finally, a single king ruled over the newly established

---

9. This is according to the *Ankokuzan jukamoku ki*, an engraved stone monument erected in 1427 upon completion of the gardens. It is the oldest extant monument in Okinawa.

independent nation. Shuri Castle, occupying the pinnacle of all *gusuku* fortresses, became the royal seat of the Ryukyu Kingdom.

The next year, Shō Hashi sent an envoy to the Ming emperor Xuande to convey the following message: "In our Ryukyu Kingdom, for over one hundred years, three kings have engaged in incessant war, causing the people to suffer greatly. I could not bear to see this situation, so I raised an army and pacified Han'anchi in the north, and then subjugated Taromii in the south. Now, peace reigns in the world, and the life of the nation has calmed. I report this to Your Majesty." The emperor responded, "Your actions align with my heart's desires. Now, do not become proud. Honor your original intentions and stabilize your nation. May your descendants continue to preserve this stability."[10] Clearly, he was more than pleased to see Ryukyu's unification, offering no rebuke for the defeat of his tributary vassals, Sanhoku and Sannan.

Thus, the diplomatic ties that Sanhoku and Sannan had nurtured with China were absorbed into the unified government, establishing the Chūzan king—that is, the Ryukyuan king, as the sole diplomatic authority of the kingdom. In this sense, Shō Hashi's unification project meant that diplomatic authority was also centralized. Furthermore, before unification, the title "Ryukyu Chūzan king" just referred to one of the three Sanzan kings. After unification, however, it became a title for the monarch of the kingdom and remained in use until the kingdom's final collapse. In fact, "Chūzan king" and "Chūzan" just became alternate titles for the king of Ryukyu and Ryukyu itself, respectively.

At long last, after three hundred years of rivalry among the *aji* chiefs, an independent and unified Ryukyu Kingdom had emerged.

---

10. *Chūzan seifu* (Genealogy Book of Chūzan). This work is an official history of the Ryukyu Kingdom compiled by a group of scholar-officials led by Sai Taku between 1697 and 1701.

CHAPTER II

Defining Characteristics of Ryukyuan History

At this point, Ryukyuan history can be set into a framework of three historically important themes.

First, once a distinctive kingdom had been established, *Ryukyu as kingdom* embarked on its own path. Secondly, unification centralized the kingdom's foreign diplomacy with China, and firmly established its position as *Ryukyu within the system of tributary nations*. Third, as the kingdom's relationship with the Chinese world empire grew and deepened, its place as *Ryukyu within Asia* became tangible. Of these, the latter two require elaboration.

Ryukyu within the system of tributary nations: When Satto accepted Yang Zai's invitation to send his younger brother Taiki as an envoy, it was in effect a declaration of intent to join the ranks of China's tributary states. Afterwards, Satto sent envoys and tribute missions every year, and as mentioned earlier, both the kings of Sanhoku and Sannan also established similar relations with China. The issue of formal "investiture" first arose in 1396, when Satto died and his son Bunei succeeded him. The *Annals of the Ming Dynasty* record that in the second month of 1404, an envoy came from Bunei, the "crown prince of Chūzan," to report the death of his father, and to request investiture. The emperor sent Shi Zhong as his investiture envoy in the same year, and Bunei was duly appointed as the "Ryukyu Chūzan king." In essence, investiture imbued a ruler with the authority to govern in the Chinese emperor's name. Shi Zhong was the first investiture envoy to visit Ryukyu, although he apparently also visited Sannan that year to invest Sannan's King Ōōso.

During the Sanzan period, investiture envoys had been sent to King Shishō in Chūzan and to King Taromii in Sannan, but after the establishment of the unified dynasty, the first investiture envoy was Chai Shan, dispatched for Shō Hashi. Later missions were sent exclusively

Table 1. **Successions during the Sanzan Period**

Chūzan		Sanhoku		Sannan	
1372	Satto initiates tribute	1383	Hanishi initiates tribute	1380	Shōsattō initiates tribute
1404	Bunei investiture			1405	Ōōso sends tribute
1406	Royal succession changes	1395	Min sends tribute	1414	Taromii enthroned
1407	Shishō investiture	1396	Han'anchi sends tribute	1415	Taromii investiture
1416	Sanhoku annexed				
1422	Shō Hashi enthroned				
1425	Shō Hashi investiture				
1429	Sannan annexed				

to the "Ryukyu Chūzan Kingdom"—that is, the Ryukyu Kingdom, and they continued until the collapse of the kingdom. The status of *Ryukyu within the system of tributary nations* was assured because when it came to diplomatic relations, the rulers of the Ryukyu Kingdom were recognized under the name of the Chinese emperor. As a result, this meant Ryukyu centered its foreign relations around its ties with China. The kingdom chose to take up its position in this "community of shared destiny" structured by Chinese policies. In addition, the tributary nations were required in all official contexts to use the Chinese imperial era name as given in the *Datong li*, a Ming almanac supplied annually by the emperor.

As a result, the history of Okinawa, which retained "original Japanese culture," set out on its own long, unique path of change. After the kingdom's establishment, its color would take on even more of a Chinese hue as Chinese influence expanded in the islands.

Ryukyu within Asia: The expansion of foreign relations, which earlier had been budding, became more prominent with the beginning of the Gusuku period, especially during the reigns of Satto and Shō Hashi. Ryukyu made its debut into international society when it joined the system of tributary nations. This is because the system was not merely a bilateral relationship between the powerful suzerain Ming dynasty and its tribute-paying vassal, but also provided a network of ties between the various tributary nations. Ryukyu took advantage of this network to engage in active diplomatic relations and trade with Korea and the nations of Southeast Asia. This topic is discussed further in Chapter 3.

In this way, the establishment of a unified dynasty under Shō Hashi's hand gave Ryukyu the form of a kingdom with deep ties to China, and further imbued it with significance as it expanded into the international community of Asia.

The Fall of the First Shō Dynasty

Following Shō Hashi's death, the dynasty he had established did not follow a smooth trajectory. As Table 2 shows, the reigns of the kings after Shō Hashi were relatively short, with Shō Toku's nine-year reign being the longest and Shō Kinpuku's four years being the shortest. Overall, the average was only about six years. Moreover, over the course of seven kings, the last, Shō Toku, was from the same generation as Shō Hashi's grandchildren. It's unlikely the short lifespans of all these kings were matters of mere chance. We must conclude that after losing the towering figure of Shō Hashi, the dynasty struggled to maintain stability and faced constant turmoil. Two significant events support this view.

In 1453, after the death of the fifth king, Shō Kinpuku, a succession dispute erupted between Shō Kinpuku's son and heir, Shiro, and

Shō Kinpuku's younger brother, Furi, both of whom were killed in the fighting. This became known as the Shiro-Furi Disturbance. The conflict appears to have been quite large-scale, and Shuri Castle, built by Shō Hashi, was completely razed to the ground. In recent years, during excavation surveys conducted as part of the reconstruction of Shuri Castle, traces of fire damage believed to date back to this event were uncovered in the foundations of the main hall.

The second event, the Gosamaru-Amawari Rebellion, took place five years later in 1458 during the reign of the sixth king, Shō Taikyū. Amawari was a powerful figure based at Katsuren Castle in central Okinawa with ambitions to claim the throne. He eventually overcame his biggest rival Gosamaru in Nakagusuku but the king's forces were later able to defeat him in turn, and the uprising was suppressed. This event was subsequently dramatized in the traditional Okinawan *kumi odori* dance-drama *Nidō tekiuchi* (The Children's Revenge), so often performed in Okinawan theater. It is commonly accepted to portray the theme of loyalty against treachery in the retainers Gosamaru and

Table 2. **Succession of the First Shō Dynasty**

No.	Name	Reign Dates	Birth Year	Genealogy
1	Shishō	1406–21	?	Son of Samekawa Ufunushi
2	Shō Hashi	1422–39	1372	Oldest son of Shishō
3	Shō Chū	1440–44	1391	Second son of Shō Hashi
4	Shō Shitatsu	1445–49	1408	Oldest son of Shō Chū
5	Shō Kinpuku	1450–53	1398	Sixth son of Shō Hashi
6	Shō Taikyū	1454–60	1415	Seventh son of Shō Hashi
7	Shō Toku	1461–69	1441	Third son of Shō Taikyū

Source: *Chūzan seifu* (Genealogy Book of Chūzan) and others.

Amawari respectively. However, it is a mistake to interpret this story through a modern ethical framework concerning loyalty and obligation between rulers and their subjects. In Ifa Fuyū's perspective, Amawari should be considered the last classical hero, and certainly at the time there were still plenty of local chiefs with deep regional roots and a strong sense of independence.

We can assume that *aji* in many parts of Okinawa were caught up in these events and that the effects were not limited to just the main parties involved. In the end, time ran out for the First Shō dynasty.

The seventh Shō king, Shō Toku, died in 1469. Soon after, the crown prince was assassinated and the entire royal family was expelled from Shuri Castle in a coup d'état. Exactly forty years after Shō Hashi had succeeded in unifying the kingdom, his dynasty had fallen apart. With the support of the coup leaders, Kanamaru, at the time the secretary of foreign relations and trade, was installed on the throne as Shō En.

In 1471, claiming himself as "crown prince," Shō En sent an envoy to China to report the death of his "father," Shō Toku, and to request the dispatch of investiture envoys. The following year, Emperor Xianzong sent Guan Rong to bestow on "Crown Prince" Shō En the title of Ryukyu Chūzan king. In effect, Shō En presented himself as the legitimate heir of Shō Toku, just as Shishō and Shō Hashi had done after overthrowing Bunei. Though they carried the same name, the two Shō dynasties were of different lineages. The field of Ryukyuan history distinguishes between the two by referring to the line of kings founded by Shō En as the Second Shō dynasty.

The new dynasty was under pressure to drastically improve the administration of the kingdom to avoid going down the same disastrous path as their predecessors. This work was undertaken by the third king, Shō Shin.

3. The Era of King Shō Shin: Establishment of the Kingdom

The Investiture Ceremony

King Shō Shin is the most famous king in the history of the Ryukyu Kingdom. He has become a figure of legendary status, and he features prominently in the early modern collection of religious songs known as the *Omoro sōshi*. Despite our knowledge of his various accomplishments, few historical records have come down to us about Shō Shin's personal story, leaving many details shrouded in mystery.

Even the circumstances of his accession to the throne are peculiar. Shō Shin was eleven when his father, Shō En, died in the seventh month of 1476. Citing Shō Shin's youth, Shō En's younger brother, Shō Sen'i, claimed the throne as the second king. However, in an unprecedented event, an oracle declared, "It is only Shō Shin who must become king!" during a religious ceremony held the following year. Shō Sen'i promptly abdicated, and Shō Shin ascended to the throne. Ifa Fuyū speculates that this abdication had been engineered by Shō Shin's mother, Ogiyaka,[11] but the historical records are silent on the matter.

Setting aside Shō Shin's legendary status, let us return to him as a historical figure. Shō Shin was the third king of the Second Shō dynasty. However, within the system of authority conferred through investiture by the suzerain power of the Ming dynasty, he was the second king of that line, because Shō Sen'i abdicated too quickly to welcome an investiture envoy. Upon his ascension in 1477, Shō Shin named himself

---

11. Hattori Shirō, Nakasone Seizen, Hokama Shuzen, eds., *Zassan, jiten, sakuhin, jo-batsu, danwa hoka jokan* [Miscellany, Dictionary, Works, Introduction-Epilogue, Discourse and Other Talks, and Notes]. Vol. 10 of *Ifa Fuyū zenshū* [The Complete Works of Ifa Fuyū] (Tokyo: Heibonsha, 1976), 216–17.

the "crown prince of the Chūzan king" and sent an envoy to the Ming government requesting investiture. Two years later in 1479, the Ming emperor Xianzong dispatched a formal investiture mission headed by Dong Min. Thus began King Shō Shin's reign, considered the golden age of the Ryukyu Kingdom.

We know that Dong Min and his investiture mission arrived aboard a single ship. We can surmise that it was a large junk, similar to the ship that brought the investiture mission for Shō Shin's successor, Shō Sei. Records show that the vessel was about 46.7 meters in length, 9.2

Royal portrait of King Shō Shin. Photo by Kamakura Yoshitarō. Okinawa Prefectural University of Arts Library and Arts Museum.

meters wide, and 4.4 meters deep.

So, how was the grand ceremony of investiture conducted? Unfortunately, there are no records remaining of this particular ceremony, but we can construct an image of it from later examples.

The investiture mission consisted of a grand delegation of about five hundred people, including the chief envoy and the vice-envoy as leaders, plus a diverse staff of civil servants, military officers, scholars, soldiers, musicians, cooks, and more. They arrived in Naha after crossing the East China Sea, having embarked from Fuzhou (Fujian Province, China) on a vessel known as a seal ship[12] or sometimes a crown ship for the special crown it carried from the Chinese emperor. These important guests were received by high-ranking officials at the Geiontei (Pavilion of Welcoming Reception), a structure built on the harbor for the purpose of welcoming guests. The entire party then paraded through Naha to the Tenshikan (Hall of Heavenly Envoys), the guest house for visiting dignitaries, where they would stay during their six-month sojourn in Ryukyu.

The envoy's first duty was to perform a memorial ceremony at Sōgenji, a temple and royal mausoleum dedicated to the spirits of past kings. In this ceremony, the envoy read the eulogy from the Chinese emperor in honor of the late king. Once this had been carried out, the investiture ceremony could be held on a later date.

Crown made of black silk and adorned with 288 precious stones. Courtesy of the Naha City Museum of History.

---

12. So called because it carried the official seal of investiture from the emperor to the new king.

Figure 3. **Illustrations of a Tribute Ship and the Chūzan King's Investiture**

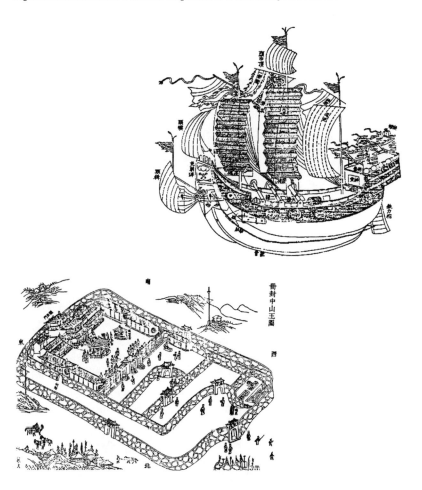

The illustration shows an investiture ceremony taking place at Shuri Castle. These drawings of King Shō Kei's investiture in 1719 were drawn by Xu Baoguang in his report *Zhongshan Chuanxinlu* (Report of an Envoy to Chūzan). University of the Ryukyus Library.

The rite of investiture took place at Shuri Castle. On that day, a representative of the Ryukyuan king would go to the Tenshikan to greet the envoy, after which they would travel in a magnificent parade from there to Shuri Castle. The dazzling splendor of this procession must have given the people of Ryukyu a clear sense of the grandeur of the Great Ming world empire. The crown prince (in this case, Shō Shin) receiving the investiture would then meet the procession at Shuri Castle's main gate, Shureimon, to guide them into the castle (the gate itself was built during the reign of King Shō Sei).

The rite of investiture was held in the central courtyard (*u-nā*), the sacred plaza enclosed by the main hall (*seiden*), the north hall (*hokuden*), the south hall (*nanden*), and the Hōshin Gate. In front of the main hall, a small, temporary building called the *kettei* housed a display of the many gifts sent to the Ryukyuan king from the Chinese emperor. The envoy and his vice-envoy stood within this building. In front of the south hall stood another temporary structure called the *sendokudai* that served as a dais for reading the imperial decree.

Every step of the ceremony was conducted in Chinese, against a background of Chinese music. The imperial decree, read aloud from the *sendokudai*, proclaimed that "the Crown Prince Shō Shin is herewith invested as the Ryukyu Chūzan king." After receiving the seal of investiture, the now lawfully proclaimed king of Ryukyu, King Shō Shin, proceeded to the *kettei* to be presented with the crown and silk robes.

Thus, his position officially recognized by the Chinese emperor, Shō Shin was reborn as the ruler of the Ryukyu Kingdom where he was referred to as *yo no nushi* (lord of the world) or *teda* (the sun).

In 1477, Shō Shin ascended the throne at the tender age of twelve and reigned for fifty years until his death at the age of sixty-one in 1526. During his long reign, he implemented numerous transformative policies that marked significant milestones in the history of the kingdom, and cultivated what is described as the golden age of Ryukyu.

CHAPTER II

Achievement of the Aji *Residency Policy*

During King Shō Shin's reign, the policy requiring residency in Shuri, imposed as a countermeasure on the *aji* class, was of central importance. Though subordinate to royal authority, the *aji* had built *gusuku* strongholds in their domains and still held influence that was not to be underestimated. As long as their power remained unchecked, the possibility of a second Shiro-Furi Disturbance, or a second Gosamaru-Amawari Rebellion, could not be ruled out. With this in mind, Shō Shin mandated that the *aji* relocate from their home territories to live in Shuri, within close reach of the king's authority.

This may seem to have been a drastic measure, but there is no evidence in the few remaining historical records that the *aji* opposed their relocation to Shuri or attempted to rebel. They moved their families and retainers to Shuri, and likely as a result of this measure, Shuri experienced a population boom. Shuri Castle, once an isolated hilltop castle with only a few surrounding houses, now donned the robes of a bustling castle town.

However, merely moving the *aji* to Shuri was not enough. It was necessary to place them firmly under royal authority and institutionalize the perception that they only existed because there was a king. For this purpose, a court ranking system was established. Specifically, a person's social rank was indicated by the color of a headpiece[13] (O. *hachimachi,* J. *haku*), and by the material of a hairpin (J. *kanzashi*). According to the *Kyūyō*, an official history of the Ryukyu Kingdom compiled between 1743 and 1745, the headpiece's color indicated its wearer's rank, with blue, green, red, yellow, and purple in ascending order of status. Above purple, there were elaborate *hachimachi* in a type

---

13. This headpiece first started out as a cloth that was wrapped around the head like a turban. The cloth eventually came to be reinforced and held in shape so that it could be worn and removed in one piece.

of woven brocade known as *ukiori*. For the hairpins, gold indicated higher rank, followed by silver. Men wore these pins in a hairstyle referred to as *kata kashira*. By the early modern period, the turban-like headpiece had evolved into a more standard hat-like shape called *kanmuri* (crown) in written records. This system of hairstyles, hairpins, and headwear to indicate the status of the kingdom's elite endured for over four hundred years.

The *aji* gathered in Shuri were organized under this hierarchy, with Shō Shin, of course, determining the headwear color and hairpin material each person would be allowed to wear. In this way, the *aji* lost their distinctive regional characteristics and became little more than titled elites surrounding the king. Presumably, most of the regional *gusuku* strongholds fell out of use and were abandoned as a consequence of these measures.

Finally, the *Momourasoe no rankan no mei* (Balustrade Memorial of Shuri Castle),[14] an inscription on the stone railing in Shuri Castle's main hall, proclaims the achievements of King Shō Shin: "He appointed a thousand retainers to official posts, and assigned roles to a hundred bureaucrats." In this way, in addition to devising the social ranking system, he established a bureaucratic system of responsibilities and official appointments. The *aji* had their displays of rank and standing with their headwear and hairpins, in a hierarchy controlled by the king at the very top.

Hachimachi. Courtesy of the Ryukyu Cultural Archives, Okinawa Prefectural Board of Education.

---

14. *Momourasoe* (lit. "thousand harbor rule") was an alternative name for Shuri Castle.

That is to say, the local chiefs were fully integrated in the political and administrative structures of the Ryukyu Kingdom, serving the king who sat at the pinnacle of the Shuri royal government.

Strengthening Regional Governance

The *Kyūyō* tells us that after the *aji* had departed for Shuri, officials from Shuri were dispatched to their former districts with the "*Aji* Codes" to communicate the king's intentions. No historical records exist with descriptions of activities in those districts related to these codes. Regrettably, there is not a single clue to answer the intriguing question of whether these officials had been sent to watch for unrest in the *aji*'s home territories or if they had been sent purely to take up local administrative duties.

However, if we consider the fragmented historical records as a whole, local governance was clearly strengthened during the reign of King Shō Shin. The practicalities of this local governance will be discussed in more detail in the fourth and fifth chapters, but in short, a system developed in which local elites in every district were authorized to implement policies in the name of the king, in accordance with his directives. As a result, the reign of Shō Shin saw the establishment of a system in which the bidding of the king ruling from Shuri was heard and implemented across the entire island society, from Amami in the north to Sakishima in the south.

Of course, King Shō Shin's efforts to establish control at the local level did not go without a hitch. An example of this is the Akahachi-Hongawara Revolt that occurred in Yaeyama.

The *Momourasoe no rankan no mei* states that in the spring of 1500, "One hundred warships were sent to attack Taiheizan and established control." "Taiheizan" referred to the Miyako and Yaeyama island groups, though it came to refer only to the Miyako group in a later period. These islands already had powerful local leaders, such as Nakasone Tōyumiya on Miyako Island, and Oyake Akahachi and Hongawara of Ishigaki Island. The threat posed by King Shō Shin's moves to exert control over the local areas meant these leaders felt they only had two choices: Fully submit to royal authority as their peers had on Okinawa Island or resist and stubbornly defend their own interests to the end.

Nakasone Tōyumiya of Miyako chose the former, but Oyake Akahachi and Hongawara of Ishigaki opted for resistance. With this, King Shō Shin sent an expeditionary force to Ishigaki and with Nakasone Tōyumiya's support, quickly suppressed the revolt.

It is important to understand that King Shō Shin simultaneously eliminated local resistance and solidified regional control in this way. As he strengthened regional government control, he was able to politically unify the entire region stretching from the Amami island group, through the Okinawa group (Okinawa Island and the smaller islands around it), all the way to the Sakishima islands—ultimately creating the regional community known as "Ryukyu."

Establishing a Hierarchy of Priestesses

Another notable policy under King Shō Shin's government was the establishment of a formal hierarchy of priestesses, or divine women.

In Ryukyu, the duties of prayer and worship of deities were entirely performed by women. This is commonly known as the creed of *Onari*, in which *onari* (women) were believed to possess great spiritual power and to have the ability to protect *ekeri* (men). Women led the prayers for abundant crops and the rituals of thanksgiving for good harvests at the various events and festivals centering on agricultural rituals held throughout the year.

First, divine women assigned to oversee religious observances at the local level were installed as *noro*. Above the *noro*, women in higher-ranking roles as *ōamo* (great mother) had oversight across a wider geographical area compared to the *noro*. Titles included *Ōamo* of Miyako, *Ōamo* of Yaeyama, Kimihae, Lady of the Southern Wind of Kumejima, *Amo* of Futa-kayata of Izenajima, Aoriyae[15] of Nakijin, *Ōamo* of Naha, and more. Similar roles were established in the Amami islands as well.

Noro priestess dressed in traditional attire. Okinawa Prefectural Archives.

---

15. Aoriyae is a Ryukyuan deity associated with wind, rain, military force, and has parallels with the Japanese deity Hachiman.

Above the *ōamo* were the highest-ranking priestesses with titles that varied slightly depending on the era. These are known to have included Aoriyae, Shuri Amoshirare, Gibo Amoshirare, Uwamori, Kimi Toyomi, Shuri Ōkimi, Kimi Tsuji, Sejiara Kimi, and Mochizuki, among others. As a group, they were known as *kimigimi*, and most of them resided in Shuri, serving as central priestesses. At the pinnacle was the most significant figure, Kikoe Ōgimi (lit. "great hearing one"), also known as Toyomu Sedakako (lit. "one whose high spiritual power echoes through the world"). King Shō Shin's younger sister, Otochitono Moikane, was the first to serve as the Kikoe Ōgimi, and his daughter Manabedaru was appointed as Sasukasa. Sasukasa was a priestess role that held the highest rank during the First Shō dynasty and was associated with sea voyages.

This policy of reorganizing priestesses aimed to exert control over the common perception of their special abilities in the world of religious ritual. It introduced a clear hierarchy within the female priesthood that was a counterpart to the central versus regional and upper versus lower divisions seen among male government officials.

Multiple Royal Construction Projects

In addition to the business of consolidating the kingdom's administrative structure, King Shō Shin undertook numerous construction projects. The list of projects undertaken during his reign is too long to give here, but, for example, in 1494, next to Shuri Castle, he founded Enkakuji, developing it into the foremost Buddhist temple in Ryukyu. He had stone shrines installed for native rituals at important sacred sites like Ben-no-utaki (Bengatake) and Sonohyan-utaki, and ordered the construction of a new royal mausoleum, the Tama-udun. The main hall at Shuri Castle had a magnificent high balustrade built with blue-tinged tuff imported from China adorning its base. Finally, in typical King Shō Shin style, a pair of great dragon pillars flanked the main steps leading up to the hall's entrance. In the later years of his reign, he built the Madama-michi (pearl road), a stone-paved road lined with pine trees on either side. The road connected Shuri Castle with the port of Naha, allowing for the deployment of soldiers to defend against the threat of pirates.

In a reflection of all these construction projects, around Shuri Castle there are numerous inscriptions commemorating King Shō Shin's achievements. The *Momourasoe no rankan no mei*, carved in large characters on the main hall's high stone railing, is well known. This inscription praises Shō Shin as a great king who stabilized the kingdom, achieved great deeds, and introduced Chinese imperial culture to codify Ryukyuan court life. Undoubtedly, King Shō Shin's reign was a transformative era that consolidated the structure of the kingdom and strengthened the authority of the king at its head.

4. Toward an Era of Change

Invasion by the Satsuma Army

Upon the death of King Shō Shin, the Second Shō dynasty continued with Shō Sei, Shō Gen, Shō Ei, and Shō Nei ascending to the throne in succession. In contrast to the First Shō dynasty, which fell into turmoil after the death of its vaunted founder, Shō Hashi, the Second Shō dynasty proceeded with no succession disputes or uprisings by powerful elites after the loss of King Shō Shin.

However, the Second Shō dynasty would soon confront difficulties from an unexpected source. After a long period of strife and unrest, Oda Nobunaga, Toyotomi Hideyoshi, and Tokugawa Ieyasu had gained control of nearly all of Japan, and established a feudal state backed by their powerful military forces. The repercussions of this change began to be felt in the Ryukyu Kingdom. In addition, the neighboring Satsuma domain, which had long maintained friendly relations with Ryukyu, began to strengthen its control over its own territory, and started using its power to make various demands of the kingdom. The second half of the sixteenth century, after King Shō Shin's death, was a difficult period for Ryukyu in its relations with Japan.

Representative of this challenging time was the demand that the kingdom participate in Toyotomi Hideyoshi's Korean campaigns during the Imjin War (1592–97). Hideyoshi and Satsuma cooperated to aggressively demand seven thousand men and ten months' worth of military provisions, in addition to financial support for building Nagoya Castle,[16] intended as a forward base for Hideyoshi's expeditions to Korea. Ryukyu, as an independent nation, struggled with these unreasonable demands. Fearing retaliation if it flat out refused to comply, Ryukyu agreed to some of the demands, but refused most of them.

Subsequently, Tokugawa Ieyasu, once he had become the sole ruler of Japan, sought Ryukyu's mediation to repair Japan's relationship with China, damaged by Hideyoshi's invasions of Korea during the Imjin War. When Ryukyu prevaricated and did not fully comply with this request, Satsuma, acting on Ieyasu's behalf and under the pretext of addressing the kingdom's years of "disrespect" with military force, sent three thousand soldiers to Ryukyu in the spring of 1609. Armed with guns and tempered by the long years of military conflict, the powerful Satsuma forces found no resistance from the Ryukyuan side. The conflict ended almost before it started, and the kingdom's territory fell under the control of the Satsuma forces in what is known as the Shimazu Invasion.

---

16. Not to be confused with Nagoya Castle (名古屋城) in Aichi Prefecture. This Nagoya Castle (名護屋城) was built in what is now Saga Prefecture.

Figure 4. **Succession of the Second Shō Dynasty**

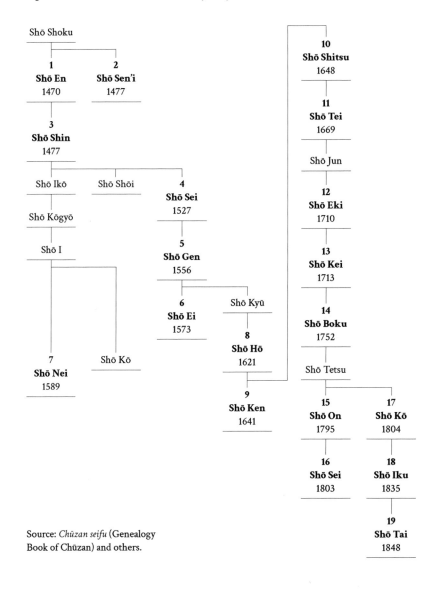

Source: *Chūzan seifu* (Genealogy Book of Chūzan) and others.

A strong popular belief holds that a disarmament policy during King Shō Shin's reign, as the kingdom sought to become a "nation of peace," was the cause of Ryukyu's rapid defeat by Satsuma. That inscription on the main hall's stone railing, the *Momourasoe no rankan no mei*, serves as the historical reference at the base of this idea, but a close reading of the relevant section translates as ". . . succeeded in exclusively acquiring swords and bows and arrows as tools for the protection of the nation." In other words, it meant the readying of armaments, including swords and bows and arrows, to protect the nation in times of emergency. Nowhere does it mention becoming a "nation of peace," or that all weapons had been abolished. Certainly, the government's weapons policy meant that the crews of Japanese traders visiting Ryukyu had their weapons taken into custody at Naha, to be returned when they departed for home. As will be discussed further in Chapter 5, Ryukyu had its own military force and was armed with all the standard weaponry.

Lacking a strong desire to fight was only one of several factors that led to Ryukyu's easy defeat by Satsuma. Satsuma's military might was also overwhelmingly superior to that of Ryukyu. In addition, the King Shō Shin-era structural and administrative reforms that had moved the *aji* class to Shuri had resulted in a government bureaucracy staffed by civil officials with very few armed retainers among them. Finally, the Ryukyu Kingdom had zero experience in foreign warfare.

Transition to Early Modern Ryukyu

With the invasion and conquest by the Satsuma military forces, the Ryukyu Kingdom lost its independence. The Amami island group (Amami Ōshima, Kikaijima, Tokunoshima, Okinoerabujima, Yorontō, and others) was separated and came under Satsuma's direct control, and the kingdom was obligated to pay Satsuma the *shinobose* annual tax, a type of vassal tribute. Satsuma exerted its control over the kingdom by permanently stationing its own magistrate in Naha to directly monitor and supervise Ryukyu, reserving the authority to appoint members of the royal council and other high-ranking posts, including the king.

Despite these measures, Satsuma did not have exclusive control over the fate of the Ryukyu Kingdom. It was itself subject to the authority of the powerful shogunate, and Satsuma's rule over Ryukyu was regulated by the *bakufu* (lit. "tent government," i.e., the shogunate itself). Historians refer to the early modern state of Japan, when the shogunate held supreme power, as the *bakuhan* (lit. "tent domain," i.e. the shogunate feudal system). In accordance with this terminology, we can understand that the Ryukyu Kingdom had been placed into the context of the national *bakuhan* system and its regulations, with Satsuma serving as its direct administrative authority.

Another factor limiting Satsuma from doing as it pleased was the continued existence of the Ryukyu Kingdom. Although it was now subordinate to the authority of Satsuma and the shogunate, the royal system persisted, and day-to-day administration was still managed by the Shuri royal government. This meant that without the cooperation of the Shuri royal government, Satsuma would not be able to achieve its aims within the kingdom. Furthermore, the kingdom's traditional tributary relationship with China remained intact, so the king continued to receive the Chinese emperor's rite of investiture. In this one area, the Ryukyuan side retained a measure of autonomy.

Had Satsuma simply broken apart the kingdom and incorporated its territory, administering it at the same level as the rest of its domain, the subsequent history of Ryukyu would certainly have been completely different. One of the reasons why Satsuma could not completely absorb Ryukyu, however, was the substantial significance of Ryukyu's long history as a distinct nation.

Historians have coined the phrase "a foreign nation within the Japanese *bakuhan* system" to capture this scenario of Ryukyu as a kingdom subordinate to the Satsuma domain and the Tokugawa shogunate, while maintaining its royal government administration as well as its position as an independent member of the Chinese imperial system of tributary nations. The period of transition into "a foreign nation within the Japanese *bakuhan* system" after the Shimazu Invasion is known as Ryukyu's early modern era.

So, what should we call the preceding period of its existence as an independent nation?

The approximately five hundred year-long stretch of time starting with the transformative Gusuku era, when local chiefs struggled with each other for control, followed by the tripartite Sanzan period, the first unified dynasty established by Shō Hashi, the kingdom's consolidation under King Shō Shin, and the final years of deteriorating relations with Japan, all the way up to the eve of the Shimazu Invasion, is a series of eras marked by events that led to the formation and development of the Ryukyu Kingdom. When viewed as a whole, this important period, corresponding to Japan's medieval period, is referred to as *Ko Ryukyu* or ancient Ryukyu as proposed by Ifa Fuyū, to distinguish it from early modern Ryukyu.

The people of Okinawa, who began their history by embracing "proto-Japanese culture," ultimately achieved a unique kingdom that was clearly distinct from the Japanese state. Ancient Ryukyu was an era of great significance in this process of evolution.

Thus far, the discussion has been little more than a series of static vignettes depicting ancient Ryukyu. This period was significant in establishing this unique kingdom and it offers a mountain of topics to delve into. From among this wealth of choices, I will cover a number of important issues for further exploration in the following chapters.

CHAPTER III
RYUKYU IN ASIA

CHAPTER III

1. The Theater of Engagement

Ryukyu under the Tributary System

The well-spring of energy that brought the Ryukyu Kingdom into existence during the era of ancient Ryukyu also extended toward Asia.

As discussed earlier, the Ming dynasty, established in 1368, faced the outside world with a foreign policy that arranged its neighbors into what may be called a system of investiture and tribute. The Ming emperor recognized the kings of these nations, bestowing his authority on them by granting investiture (in the form of an official seal), and in return these kings sent messengers with written declarations and goods to show their allegiance.[1] The aim was to create a world order by forging diplomatic ties in a system where foreign nations were subordinate to the Chinese emperor at the top, that is, the Chinese imperial suzerain-vassal system.

One key point of this policy was that ships from nations outside the system of tributary nations were denied entry into Chinese ports, specifically as protection against the devastating forces of *wakō* pirates who raided the Chinese coast during this period. The year after Emperor Hongwu founded the Ming dynasty, he quickly dispatched an envoy to Japan with an official letter announcing the new dynasty and its intentions, along with a strongly worded request to suppress the *wakō*. Notably, this first envoy to Japan was Yang Zai, who would

---

1. In Japanese, this is referred to as *shinkō* (paying tribute), or *chōkō* (sending tribute).

later be the first envoy to visit Ryukyu and urge King Satto to join the tributary nations. Japan, in a state of political unrest, was slow to meet the Ming dynasty's demands. However, the Ming continued to press the Japanese side, with the hope that if Japan joined the system of tributary nations, the problem of the raiding *wakō* might be resolved. In 1401, hoping to seize control of foreign relations, the shogun of the Muromachi *bakufu*, Ashikaga Yoshimitsu, sent emissaries as the "king of Japan" to the Ming emperor with a selection of tribute offerings. The following year, Emperor Jianwen sent an envoy mission to perform the ritual of investiture to recognize Yoshimitsu as "king of Japan." In this way, Japan, too, became a member of the system of tributary nations.

Though there were some variations in circumstances between the different nations, their primary objective in being granted investiture and tributary status was to gain access to trade with China. By any metric, China was the world's most powerful nation at this time, and it was also the world's largest producer of commodities. Many countries willingly accepted the absolute authority of the Ming emperor in their endeavors to acquire highly desirable Chinese goods. From the reign of Emperor Hongwu through to that of Emperor Yongle (from the late fourteenth century to the early fifteenth), the Ming imperial tributary system reached not only East Asia and Southeast Asia, but as far as South Asia, Central Asia, Western Asia, and even parts of Africa.

Debut in the International Community of East Asia

The Ming dynasty designated the ports of entry for each country and the Maritime Trade Office oversaw the entry and exit of foreign vessels. The port designated for Ryukyu was at Quanzhou in Fujian Province, Japan went to Ningbo in Zhejiang, and the nations of Southeast Asia and westward went to Guangdong in Guangzhou. In their assigned port of Quanzhou, the Ryukyuans were provided with a dedicated facility for their use, the Rai'en'eki (Quanzhou Ryukyu House). When the shipping office was relocated to the city of Fuzhou in 1472, the Ryukyuans were given the Jū'en'eki (Fuzhou Ryukyu House)[2] there. As the word "eki" (station) implies, these facilities were part of China's domestic postal system and served as windows into the country for foreign nations. However, not even nations that paid tribute were allowed to move freely outside their designated ports.

The Ming dynasty also established a timetable for tribute missions that determined how frequently each tributary nation could make voyages to China. According to the *Da Ming hui dian* (Collected Statutes of the Ming Dynasty), Annam (Vietnam) and Java had a cycle of one mission every three years, while Japan was permitted one mission every ten years.

On top of the sharp access restrictions China imposed on visiting traders in search of Chinese goods, the Ming dynasty also implemented a ban on maritime travel for the Chinese population. The ban, a form of isolationism, was intended to prevent coastal inhabitants from aiding the *wakō*, or from even going to sea and becoming raiders themselves. As a result, Chinese merchants engaged in overseas trade suffered a significant setback, and those who ignored the ban had no choice but to engage in smuggling and clandestine trading.

The two policies, the tributary system and the ban on maritime travel, resulted in a drastic reduction in official channels for supplying Chinese commodities to foreign markets. This reduction was because of the Ming policy of not authorizing trade with nations that were outside the tributary system. Even member nations within the system could only visit their designated ports according to their

---

2. These overseas institutions are also referred to as Ryukyu-kan (琉球館). A Ryukyu-kan was also maintained in Satsuma domain for relations with Japan.

tribute schedule, making it difficult to obtain goods freely. And of course, Chinese merchants themselves were strictly prohibited from conducting maritime trade.

This situation offered an unprecedented opportunity for any country in medieval East Asia that was a member of the tributary nations system, had easy access to Chinese commodities, and could fill the enormous gap left by the Chinese commercial powers that had vanished in the wake of the maritime travel ban. The nation that had the momentum generated by its own national formation, and thus was able to thoroughly take advantage of this opportunity, was the newly established Ryukyu Kingdom on the eastern edge of the East China Sea.

After King Satto of Chūzan dispatched the first tribute mission to China in 1372, Ryukyu had enjoyed a tribute timetable of one mission a year and in some years, two missions. They had established a position that allowed them to send trade ships to China annually, ensuring their access to great quantities of Chinese commodities. King Shō Hashi's unification of the kingdom let them further expand their tribute trade. This led to the emergence of a robust ocean trade route that spanned the East China Sea between Ryukyu and Fujian, allowing for the flow of a vast amount of Chinese goods. Beginning in the 1470s, Ryukyu's tribute missions were limited to one mission every two years, but they still held a remarkably advantageous position compared to other countries. Historian Akiyama Kenzō notes that over the course of the Ming era (1368–1644), Ryukyu ranked first for tribute missions at 171 trips, a decisive lead compared to Annam in second place with 89 missions. Other nations included Siam (Thailand) in sixth place with 73 missions, Korea in tenth place with 30, Malacca (Melaka) in twelfth place with 23 missions, and finally Japan in thirteenth place with 19 missions.[3]

---

3. Akiyama Kenzō, *Nis-Shi kōshōshi kenkyū* [Research on the History of Sino-Japanese Cultural Interactions] (Tokyo: Iwanami Shoten, 1939), 552.

CHAPTER III

As the Hub of "The Silk Road of the Sea"

Around this time in history, Chinese products were highly competitive and sought after, with people around the world always eager for more. The ability to acquire large quantities of these desirable goods via the tribute and trade route under the Ming dynasty's framework of policies immediately boosted Ryukyu's status as a commercial power. Ryukyu itself, of course, was not a large consumer of all these Chinese products. Only a small portion of the total was kept for domestic consumption while the rest was loaded onto trading ships and delivered to ports in Japan, Korea, and the various nations of Southeast Asia.

Consider the map of the Ryukyu Kingdom's trade routes on the following page. Spanning from East Asia to Southeast Asia, these far-flung routes were established primarily to procure Chinese goods and supply them to other countries. Ryukyu played the leading part in pioneering this "Silk Road of the Sea," which might also be called the "Porcelain Road" for its main trade commodity of Chinese ceramics.

In the previous chapter, we saw that in addition to seeing Ryukyuan history through the frameworks of *Ryukyu as kingdom* and *Ryukyu within the system of tributary nations*, Shō Hashi's unification of the kingdom added a third perspective, which, specifically with these international trading ventures in mind, I call *Ryukyu within Asia*. In sum, by becoming a tributary vassal of the Ming dynasty and thus gaining access to much sought-after Chinese commodities, the Ryukyu Kingdom made its dramatic debut into the international community of Asia through trade.

Yet, how was Ryukyu able to buy such large quantities of Chinese goods? It's clear that the cargo of ships returning from China would consist mainly of Chinese goods. So too was the case for ships sailing to Japan, Korea, and Southeast Asian countries. But exactly what kind of cargo were ships from Ryukyu carrying when they crossed the East China Sea to China?

Figure 5. **Trade Routes of the Ryukyu Kingdom**

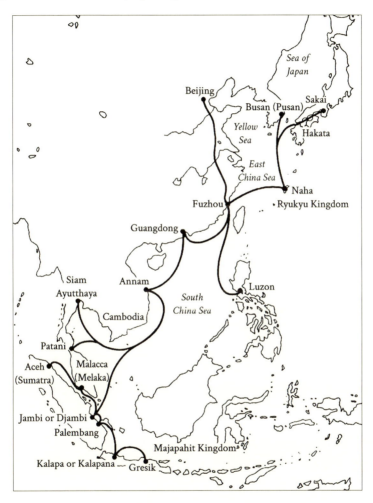

This map is based on diplomatic documents such as the *Rekidai hōan* compiled in the mid-early modern period. According to the *Rekidai hōan*, ships sent to Southeast Asia between about 1424 and 1570 included 58 to Siam, 20 to Malacca, and 11 to Patani, among others. These are the recorded instances, and the actual numbers are assumed to have been even higher. Furthermore, the route to Beijing from Fuzhou during this period used the Grand Canal.

CHAPTER III

Bridge of Nations Bell. Courtesy of the Okinawa Prefectural Museum & Art Museum.

A list of the tribute goods offered by Ryukyu found in the *Collected Statutes of the Ming Dynasty* includes horses, shells, textiles, cowhides, sulfur, and more items that were clearly sourced in Ryukyu. At the time, many horses and cows were bred in Ryukyu; horses would serve as pack animals while cattle were skinned for their hides which were tanned before export to China. The shells, especially green turban, were valued for their iridescent mother-of-pearl, a material used for inlays in lacquerware. The textiles were a light summer cloth produced in Ryukyu, presumably similar to modern *bashōfu*, a banana-fiber cloth. Sulfur, the base ingredient in gunpowder, was mined in Ryukyu's Iōtorijima.[4]

However, this limited list of items could not have been sufficient to purchase large amounts of Chinese goods. A closer look at the *Collected Statutes of the Ming Dynasty* illuminates the situation further. Japanese products such as swords, tasseled fans, painted and gilded fans, copper ore, and products like ivory, tin, rosewood, and spices from Southeast Asia are also listed. Ryukyu was not only shipping goods it had produced domestically, but also goods sourced from other countries.

---

4. Iōtorijima (lit. "sulfur bird island") is a small island with the only active volcano in the Ryukyu islands. It has been uninhabited since 1958 and its last recorded eruption was in 1968.

With this, the answer to our question becomes evident. In Japan, Korea, and Southeast Asia, Ryukyuan ships traded Chinese goods for local specialty products, and then returned to Naha Port with nearly full holds. There they would add new domestic products to the load and set off for China; from there, repeating in a standard transit trade pattern, the ships departed on their rounds with their holds once again filled with Chinese goods. The trade routes of the Ryukyu Kingdom were thus established as sales routes to distribute quantities of Chinese goods, while simultaneously serving as procurement routes for products to export to China.

There is a well-known Buddhist temple bell inscribed with a passage capturing the spirit of Ryukyu during its heyday as a thriving center of the transit trade. This bell, known as the "Bridge of Nations Bell," cast in 1458, is now on display in the Okinawa Prefectural Museum & Art Museum. A section of the passage reads as follows:

> The land of Ryukyu holds an excellent position in the South Seas, collecting the excellence of Samhan [Korea], intimate with the Great Ming [China], and friendly with Jichiiki [Japan]. It emerges in the midst of these neighbors like the island of Hōrai. Traveling by ship, its people form a bridge to the ten thousand lands and fill every corner of its temples with exotic treasure.

Put simply, Ryukyu sits in a prime location in the South Seas, learning from the rich culture of Korea, intimately connected to China, and in friendly relations with Japan. The country is like the mythical island of Penglai,[5] springing up in the middle of East Asia. Its people skillfully navigate trading ships, serving as a bridge to the world, and the world's

---

5. Penglai (J. Hōrai) is a legendary mountainous island found in both Chinese and Japanese mythology.

goods fill the land. This bell on which this passage is inscribed was not hung in a temple, but in the main hall at Shuri Castle. This can be considered as the perfect expression of the Ryukyu Kingdom's pride in its status as a transit trade power stretching out far across the waters of Asia.

2. Characteristics of Overseas Trade

State-controlled Trade

How could a tiny island nation like the Ryukyu Kingdom engage in such extensive trade activities?

I have already shown how the Ming dynasty's system of investiture and tribute, as well as the ban on maritime travel, set the stage for Ryukyu's activities. In this context, it's important to note that the existence of the tributary system itself was clearly the background for Ryukyu's trade enterprises. Consider again the map on page 83. Although there were variations depending on the period, the scope of the trade routes developed by Ryukyu correspond directly with the scope of tributary nations developed by the Ming dynasty. In other words, Ryukyu's international trade grew out of the bilateral relationship between China (the suzerain state) and Ryukyu (the vassal state), which allowed the kingdom to develop relations with other tributary nations.

This is clearly laid out in the *Rekidai hōan* (Treasury of Successive Generations), a collection of Ryukyuan diplomatic papers. Written in classical Chinese over a span of 440-plus years, from 1424 to 1867, this collection contains the kingdom's official correspondence concerning foreign relations. Of note is that in addition to the majority of documents related to China, there are also *ziwen* (letters exchanged between officials of equal standing) addressed to kings and relevant ministries in Korea and Southeast Asia. A frequently recurring phrase in these papers, "for the purpose of presenting tribute to the Great Ming," pressed the point that ships were sent to procure goods for tribute to the Ming dynasty. While this might have been a way of leveraging China's authority to secure better trade deals, the phrase emphasized Ryukyu's legitimate purposes for trade and the need for cooperation between tributary nations even more.

Another characteristic of Ryukyu's overseas trade to consider is that it was a state-run enterprise managed by the king, with Shuri Castle as the center of command and the administrative headquarters. In fact, the entire country was engaged in promoting overseas trade. I believe that Ryukyu's attitude of aiming to become a trading nation was one of the reasons why its overseas trade flourished.

As symbolized by the fact that most of our information about Ryukyu's overseas trade is based on the diplomatic correspondence recorded in the *Rekidai hōan*, this trade always fundamentally involved diplomacy. For example, of the many extant communiqués addressed to the king of Malacca requesting consideration for conducting smooth business transactions in Malacca, all were directly from the king of Ryukyu himself. All personnel on board the trade ships bound for Malacca were the king's servants, and the profits from trade belonged to the king. In short, even the ships themselves were official vessels owned by the king.

Huge Tribute Ships

In Ryukyuan history, the overseas trading ships that sailed out of Naha's harbor are referred to as tribute ships. These were enormous seafaring vessels of lengths exceeding 40 meters, belonging to the lineage of Chinese junks. As seen in the previous chapter, we can imagine that

CHAPTER III

King Shō Sei's investiture envoy arrived on one of these huge ships. Interestingly, and perhaps not entirely surprising, the Ming dynasty provided Ryukyu with tribute ships for a period of time after Ryukyu joined the tribute and trade system. In the *Annals of the Ming Dynasty*, the official history of the Ming, entries note that not only were tribute ships frequently provided to Ryukyu, but that the maintenance and repair of these ships was also covered. However, by the second half of the fifteenth century, even the Ming government had to end this special arrangement on financial grounds. Ryukyu then acquired the shipbuilding technology for Fujian-style junks and started building tribute ships at its own expense.

These tribute ships were some of the most technologically advanced vessels on the seas during that era. The backbone of the ship, the keel, was laid with pine beams from stem to stern. Attached to this, holding together the ship's frame, were the ribs. Thick planks were then arranged over the entire structure of the ship to form the gunwale, or outer walls of the ship. In the interior, bulkheads partitioned the space into compartments, built so that if the hull was breached while at sea, only one room would flood. Ryukyu's possession of such superlative ships as these was an important factor in its ability to conduct international maritime trade.

It may seem obvious, but it's important to understand that just because they were called tribute ships, does not mean that these vessels were used solely for carrying tribute to China. Upon their return, these ships would set sail again, this time with Chinese goods bound for other countries. In reality, these tribute ships were simply merchant trade ships plying the entirety of the transit trade routes.

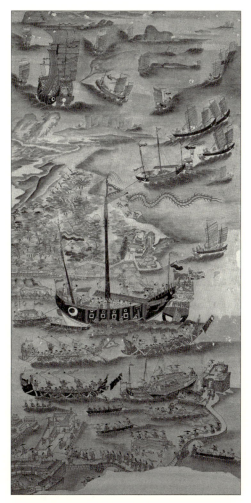

A tribute ship from the Ryukyu Kingdom leaving for Ming China. Courtesy of the Okinawa Prefectural Museum & Art Museum.

CHAPTER III

Kumemura: Immigrant Community of Experts

The people of Kumemura, or the "thirty-six families of people from Min," were another powerful force supporting Ryukyu's overseas trade. Min is a colloquial term for Fujian Province, and the so-called thirty-six families meant "people with a multitude of family names." As this designation implies, this neighborhood was settled by numerous Chinese immigrants who came to Ryukyu from Fujian Province. The area near Naha Port was first called Tōei (China camp). While still pronounced as Tōei in Japanese, the characters were later changed to mean "China glory." Eventually, the area became known as Kumemura.

The residents of Kumemura did not all arrive at once. Rather, it is likely that even before Chūzan's King Satto started sending tribute, a small number of Chinese people lived in Naha and their numbers probably increased as the tribute trade prospered. Others would come to provide technical expertise in response to requests from the Ryukyu Kingdom. In their later years, some of these ethnic Chinese would express their desire to live out their remaining years in their ancestral home and thus return to China. In a sense, this shows that these individuals were officially recognized as migrants by both the Ryukyuan and Chinese sides. For the most part, however, we can assume that many of the people in Kumemura had come there in violation of the ban on maritime travel, but there are few cases of the Ming government raising complaints against Ryukyu regarding these offenders.

The kingdom welcomed these people and placed them into positions of responsibility. Just being from a more technologically advanced society made the residents of Kumemura and their know-how indispensable to Ryukyu's overseas trading. Whether in matters of shipbuilding, ship repair and maintenance, navigation, interpretation, drafting diplomatic documents, trade techniques, information from abroad, and more, their professional skills and knowledge were key in administering the overseas trade venture, and an important consideration for the kingdom was how to utilize them most effectively. The diplomatic records in the *Rekidai hōan* were in fact the work of the Kumemura residents. Furthermore, the delegations dispatched to different countries aboard the tribute ships—many in key positions such as deputy leaders and official interpreters and even the crew sailing the vessel—were mainly from Kumemura.

Kumemura itself, however, was not integrated into the administration of the Ryukyu Kingdom as an official part of the Shuri royal government, instead maintaining a degree of autonomy relative to the government. In the following years, an official position known as the chief of Kumemura (its leading administrator, or mayor) was established. This official oversaw several staff positions and supervised a unique system that had, in effect, the nature of an independent residential district. The royal government employed these Chinese residents in the business of overseas trading, making effective use of their professional skills in the process.

Wang Mao, who served as state minister for Shishō, the founder of the first Shō dynasty, and Huai Ji, who was very active as state minister to the second king, Shō Hashi, were both ethnic Chinese. Similarly, among the residents of Kumemura, there were those who were not merely overseas trade professionals, but who were also directly involved in Ryukyuan state politics. Despite the importance of these Kumemura residents, however, they did not manage Ryukyu's overseas trade directly, nor did they represent the kingdom to other countries. Even when figures like Wang Mao and Huai Ji were active, they did not become the leaders of Shuri Castle and represent the national government. The Ryukyuan king remained the central figure of the trade enterprise, and he alone continued to wield power from his seat at the head of the government. In other words, Kumemura operated as a team of contractors, and it was the king himself who commissioned their services.

CHAPTER III

Private Trade within Official Trade

What, then, were the merits in supporting Ryukyu's overseas trade for the residents of Kumemura? To understand this question, we need to take a closer look at the actual practices of Ryukyu's trade (its tribute trade) with China.

The tribute missions followed a set pattern. Having crossed the East China Sea, they would enter the Min River, navigating through the rocky reef barrier called the "Gate of Five Tigers," and then continue westward upriver to finally arrive in Fuzhou. The delegation of several hundred Ryukyuans would stay at the Jū'en'eki (Fuzhou Ryukyu House), with a group of about twenty continuing inland toward the capital at Beijing under official Chinese escort. There they would stay at the Huitongguan (J. Kaidōkan), a guesthouse for foreign visitors. On the appointed day they would be granted an audience with the emperor at the Forbidden City to present documents and tribute items from the king of Ryukyu; in return, the emperor bestowed letters and appropriate gifts to the king and others. Gifts and souvenirs in hand, the delegation would then set out on the return journey to Fuzhou, rejoin their team awaiting them at the Jū'en'eki, and together board the tribute ship to return home.

At what point in this pattern of events did any trading take place? There was some trade with designated merchants during the stay at the Huitongguan in Beijing, but this was only on a small scale, a minor part of the overall tribute trade. The heart of the trading took place at the Jū'en'eki in Fuzhou, between the Ryukyu House traders and designated merchants, and it was these transactions that determined the profits and losses of the tribute trade. When Fuzhou merchants did not have goods that the Ryukyuans wanted, they worked through their business network to acquire them from other regions of China. The vast majority of the dealings at the Huitongguan and at the Ryukyu House in Fuzhou were conducted on behalf of the Shuri royal government, by royal retainers working busily to oversee the trading. The process included compiling a list of all the items purchased in China for submission to the Maritime Trade Office, and apparently, for the most part, the Chinese authorities granted tax exemptions and allowed the goods to be exported.

In cooperating with this state-run enterprise, did the people of Kumemura share in the profits of this trading? While the historical records do not tell us much on the matter, it's possible to infer from later circumstances that there were other ways to earn income.

Since privately-owned cargo was permitted on the official tribute ships, one method was to bring commodities that could be sold for a profit in Fuzhou. This approach was not limited to the Kumemura residents; the Ryukyuans aboard were also permitted to carry goods for sale as a kind of benefit for "overseas travelers." This was because there was nothing resembling travel expense accounts as we would know them today, and this provided a measure of security in case those aboard encountered any dangers during the voyage. Even today in Okinawa, the term *Tō tabi* (Tang journey), or making the voyage to China, is a euphemism for dying. As a consequence, in addition to carrying the royal government's official trade goods on the round trips across the East China Sea, the ships also included private cargo. In other words, the official trade enterprise known as the tribute trade also included a system of private trade. This in turn helped maintain the official trade enterprise.

As far as the Kumemura residents who had violated the maritime travel ban to emigrate to Ryukyu were concerned, the Ming government's official endorsement of the tribute trade allowed them to engage in private, non-governmental commerce in which they excelled. This was the attraction in supporting Ryukyu's tribute trade.

CHAPTER III

Private Trade on the Arrival of Investiture Envoys

The investiture envoys who came to Ryukyu as messengers from the Chinese emperor had a similar arrangement. The chief envoy, the deputy envoy, and others appointed by the emperor to lead the envoy mission, would travel from Beijing to Fuzhou to begin preparations for the crossing to Ryukyu. At this point, a ship might be newly built, or an existing civilian vessel might be appropriated and suitably refitted. Though traveling to Ryukyu on official state business, the ship carrying the delegation of five hundred people including investiture envoys was also laden with large quantities of trade goods. These privately-owned goods were carried because, due to the dangers involved, some form of personal benefit was necessary to compensate the public officials dispatched on such missions. The seal ship (the ship carrying the investiture envoy) also carried cargo consisting of goods belonging to the many Fujianese personnel on board. This was because these missions would not be possible without the efforts of these personnel, including the building or chartering of the seal ships, as well as their operation during the voyage, and more. They, too, were essential members of the delegation. From the perspective of the Fujianese support staff, this was their opportunity to engage in private trading on a grand scale under the auspices of a nationally sanctioned investiture envoy mission.

In Ryukyu, the goods, which came to be known as "Chinese cargo goods," would be appraised, with Ryukyuan officials in effect setting a price after an inspection, and then usually buying the entire lot. Since there were no civilian merchants in Ryukyu, the task of purchasing goods fell to the Shuri royal government. In this way, the private trading that took place within the Ryukyuan tribute missions was paralleled by private trading by the members of the investiture delegations. This means that while the trading between Ryukyu and

China was fundamentally a public, official enterprise (the tribute trade), we must recognize that it incorporated and relied on private trading as well.

The Chinese Network

This perspective is also important in considering Ryukyu's trade with Southeast Asia. For example, the records in the *Rekidai hōan* are of course written in classical Chinese, but why were the letters addressed to different nations in Southeast Asia also written in Chinese? Why were the communiqués from kings in Southeast Asia to the king of Ryukyu also expressed in Chinese? Further, among those traveling to Southeast Asia, why were the translators all Chinese-speaking Kumemura residents? This line of questioning brings the background of the Ryukyuan overseas trade into a clearer view.

Prior to the maritime travel ban, many Chinese emigrants had established settlements in trade ports all over Southeast Asia and built dynamic trading operations based in their respective port cities. Like the residents of Kumemura in Ryukyu, these overseas Chinese were predominantly from Fujian Province. As pointed out earlier, however, no matter how they had come to be involved in the merchant trade between Southeast Asia and China, enforcement of the maritime travel ban must have dealt a serious blow to their livelihoods. Smuggling aside, just as in Ryukyu, participating in the tribute trade of their local government was likely their primary means of restoring profit.

As a result, among these overseas Chinese there must have been those who occupied positions as consultants to their local government in matters pertaining to diplomacy and trade. Doubtless there were others who worked as shipbuilders, navigators, writers of diplomatic communications, and translators in support of local governments. Put simply, these overseas Chinese residents in every trading port served as a cadre of experts who were able to manage the trade ships arriving from Ryukyu, and they cooperated with their counterparts from Kumemura to facilitate trade between Ryukyu and Southeast Asia.

A look at the exchanges between Ryukyu and Palembang clearly shows a relationship between the local Chinese and the Kumemura residents. The Majapahit Empire (1293–ca. 1527), based in neighboring Java Island, nominally governed Palembang[6] but was unable to establish real control over it, allowing the overseas Chinese residents there to gain dominance and achieve political independence. At that time, the leader of the Chinese community also led tribute missions to Ming China and engaged in the tribute trade. The trade between Ryukyu and Palembang began in response to these conditions. Further, according to the *Rekidai hōan*, it was Huai Ji, Shō Hashi's political advisor, who played the central role in initiating the Palembang trade from the Ryukyuan side. The Ryukyu-Palembang trade makes clear the relationship between the overseas Chinese residents in Ryukyu and those in Palembang.

The use of classical Chinese in official international correspondence and the widespread use of Chinese as a lingua franca was due to this network of Chinese people. This means that communities like Kumemura, located near the port of Naha, were not unique to Ryukyu, but instead Kumemura was simply one of many typical overseas Chinese communities scattered throughout the Southeast Asian world.

---

6. In historical records, Palembang was referred to as Jiugang (lit. "old port") and is located on the island of Sumatra in modern-day Indonesia.

Transformation of the Korea Trade

Considering the trade between Ryukyu, Korea, and Japan through the lens of trading by private individuals provides a useful perspective.

Relations between Ryukyu and Korea began in 1389 when King Satto of Chūzan sent home several Koreans who had been abducted and sold to Ryukyu by *wakō* pirates. As a goodwill gesture and seeking trade relations, he also sent along gifts including sulfur, sappanwood, and pepper. The king of Goryeo seems to have struggled with this offer as there was no precedent for relations with Ryukyu. In the end, however, he accepted Satto's request for trade, and sent an envoy mission led by Kim Yunhu to convey a message of gratitude. Three years later in 1392, the Goryeo dynasty fell and was replaced by the Joseon Kingdom, established by Yi Seong-gye. Despite the change in regime, exchanges continued between the two regions.

Ryukyu took the lead in the trade exchanges with Korea. This was because their focus was on selling all their Chinese and Southeast Asian trade goods in the Korean marketplaces, and they regarded the Korean markets as a source for new export products destined for China and Southeast Asia. However, the sea route for Ryukyuan trade ships heading for Korea, through waters near Kyushu and Tsushima that were busy with both private merchants and *wakō* pirates, exposed the Ryukyuan ships to frequent interference and attacks. Faced with these substantial risks, Ryukyu shifted its policy in the mid-fifteenth century and instead of sending ships directly to Korea, opted to engage in indirect trade by dealing through intermediary merchants in Kyushu and Tsushima.

This situation may be considered fatal to Ryukyu's direct trade with Korea. The *Yijo shillok* (Annals of the Yi [Joseon] Dynasty) recounts frequent incidents of private traders from Kyushu and Tsushima claiming to be Ryukyuan envoys seeking trade with

Joseon, even though the Ryukyu Kingdom had not requested such trade (known as the "False Envoy Problem"). Though the Joseon side was aware of the true identity of these "false envoys," they were concerned that refusal might cause them to turn to piracy and cause havoc along the Korean coast. Consequently, the Joseon authorities had no choice but to tacitly go along with these "envoys." Thus, direct trade between Ryukyu and Korea was reduced to mere formality quite early on, with private trade merchants in Japan coming to mediate between the two sides.

Japanese Merchants as Intermediaries

The Japanese state was not powerful enough to control these private traders; on the contrary, these private enterprises dominated along the coasts, in the island areas, and on the high seas. As a result, Ryukyu's trade with Japan was directly influenced by the power of these private traders, whom the Japanese authorities could not control. Ryukyu dispatched frequent envoys to its neighbor, the lord of Satsuma, and to the shogun of the Muromachi *bakufu*, and sent trade ships directly to places like Hakata (Fukuoka), Bōnotsu (Kagoshima), Hyōgo, and Sakai (Osaka). In all of these places, the private traders were a large and influential presence.

From quite early on, Ryukyu's Japan trade was transformed so that instead of Ryukyuan ships making direct trips to Japan, indirect trade developed in which Japanese private traders made round-trip voyages between Japan and Ryukyu. Routes between Naha and Hakata, Bōnotsu, Hyōgo, and Sakai connected Ryukyu with a robust private trade network, although there were also plenty of *wakō* among the legitimate private traders. These routes extended to include the Korea trade routes as well.

Scholar Shin Suku, representing the Joseon Kingdom, provides a description of Ryukyu in *Haedong jeguk gi* (Records of Countries across the Sea to the East, 1471) as:

> A narrow land with a dense population. They work on great ships [tribute ships] in trade. To the west, they connect with Namban [Southeast Asia] and China; to the east, they engage with Japan and our own country. The trade ships of Japan and Namban gather at the seaport of their capital. The local people set up stalls [shops] along the waterfront [port] to engage in mutual trading.[7]

He also points out how "they would send their own people directly or employ Japanese traders already in their country [Ryukyu] to do business on their behalf."

With the involvement of Japanese merchants in the Japan-Korea route, the goods brought to Naha included people who had been abducted and enslaved by *wakō* pirates. This marked Naha's start as "an important slave market in East Asia."[8] Around 1431, there were more than one hundred enslaved people in Naha who had been taken from the Korean coast. Some facts about this group are known: five of them still remained in 1456, by then elderly, and all the women had married Ryukyuan men.[9] The Naha "slave market" did not come about due to a strong demand on the Ryukyuan side. It was the result of transactions between traders who

---

7. Shin Suk-ju, *Kaitō shokoki: Chōsenjin no mita chūsei no Nihon to Ryūkyū* [Haedong Jegukgi: Korean Perspectives of Japan and the Ryukyu Islands], trans. Tanaka Takeo (Tokyo: Iwanami Shoten, 1991), 237–38. First published in 1471.
8. Tanaka Takeo, *Chūsei taigai kankeishi* [A History of Medieval Foreign Relations] (Tokyo: University of Tokyo Press, 1975), 296.
9. Higashionna Kanjun, *Higashionna Kanjun zenshū 3* [The Complete Works of Higashionna Kanjun 3] (Tokyo: Daiichi Shobō, 1979), 46, 53.

arrived in port with slaves to sell, and the visiting traders who bought them. The Ryukyuan king participated in these exchanges by buying the enslaved people, and often repatriating them to Korea.

Nevertheless, the relationship between the Ryukyu Kingdom and the Japanese traders, *wakō* included, was not antagonistic. Fundamentally, the relationship should be regarded as having been mutually complementary. This is because the Japanese market was essential in selling the great quantities of imported goods acquired through the tribute trade and the Southeast Asian trade routes; at the same time, in turn, the Japan routes were necessary as a source for export goods to carry to China and Southeast Asia. On the other hand, Japanese traders were limited in that they could not engage directly in the tribute trade themselves, and they lacked ships capable of making the voyage to Southeast Asia. However, they benefitted by bringing Japanese goods to Naha, where they had easy access to abundant Chinese and Southeast Asian goods.

On Diplomatic Relations with Japan

I have shown how the overseas trade took place in tandem with diplomacy. This calls into question the nature of Ryukyu's diplomatic relations with Japan, wherein lies an intriguing fact. The *Rekidai hōan*, the kingdom's collection of diplomatic papers, does not contain a single document indicating a relationship with Japan.

Why is that? In fact, as explained earlier, all the documents in the *Rekidai hōan* are in classical Chinese, but all the correspondence with Japan was in kana script or a mixture of kana and Chinese characters (kanji). Already at the beginning of the fifteenth century, the Ryukyuan king sent a missive to the Ashikaga shogun written entirely in kana, and the shogun replied in a letter addressed to "*Riukiu koku no yo no nushi*" (Lord of the land of Ryukyu). The use of kana script was introduced when Japanese monks came to Ryukyu around the thirteenth century. These monks residing in Ryukyu handled diplomatic relations with Japan. In other words, just as Chinese residents of Kumemura managed diplomatic matters with China, Korea, and Southeast Asia, the Japanese monks who had come to Ryukyu were involved in affairs related to Japan. Perhaps, unlike with the other countries, a sense of shared identity called for a different approach to be taken. The use of both classical Chinese and kana script in official documents is deeply connected to the writs of appointment, an issue which will be discussed in the following chapters.

Furthermore, the phrase *Yamato tabi* (Yamato journey) appears in the *Omoro sōshi*, revealing the term used for voyages to Japan.

Encounter with the Portuguese

The conditions outlined above make it clear that Ryukyu's foreign trade was not based only on official trading, but was also supported by private and civilian merchant trading that took place within and around its periphery. Perhaps the reality was that the lively private and merchant trading that had occurred before the Ming era had taken on a more flexible nature in order to adapt to the new policies of the tribute-trade system and the restrictions on maritime travel that had prioritized official, public trading. Sending trade ships to Southeast Asia became a way to expand the reach of Ryukyu's trade routes.

The Indian Ocean lies to the west of the Strait of Malacca. Established around the beginning of the fifteenth century, the flourishing Malacca Sultanate brought Arab and Indian traders across the Indian Ocean. Riding the wave of the Age of Discovery, Portugal entered the scene, and in 1511, when the Ryukyu Kingdom was at its height under the reign of King Shō Shin, Malacca was conquered by Portuguese forces. Soon after

CHAPTER III

this, a Portuguese man named Tomé Pires, who stayed in Malacca after the conquest, described in some detail the "Lequios" (Ryukyuans) in his *Account of the Lands of the East*. Pires mentioned that two or three times a year, Lequio trade ships would come into Malacca, and return home again carrying large quantities of fabric from Bengal, India.

It is no surprise that the Ryukyuans came there to do business with Indians, as it was a hub of the East-West trade. Nevertheless, it is important to note when Ryukyu extended its overseas trading routes all the way to Malacca, it was, in effect, automatically connecting to trade routes reaching further west, across the Indian Ocean to West Asia and the Mediterranean. With Malacca as intermediary, Ryukyu's Southeast Asian trade linked it into a global trade network, and these transactions with Indian traders in Malacca serve as a symbolic example of that connection.

Even amidst the tumultuous conquest of the Malacca Sultanate, Portuguese forces obviously encountered Ryukyu's Southeast Asian trade. Besides Tomé Pires' *Account of the Lands of the East*, the Portuguese left many reports and maps about the Lequios. Among them was Diego de Freitas, who in 1540 recorded a variety of information he learned from the Lequios he had met and befriended in the city of Ayutthaya in Siam (modern Thailand). For example, he reports that the captains of the Lequio trade ships were obligated by the king of Ryukyu to bring back everyone who had sailed with the ship, in life or death. In fact, he witnessed three Ryukyuans, who had died in Siam, preserved in salt for their return home. Freitas also notes that Portuguese ships twice visited the island of the Lequio people. According to experts, those ships had visited in 1542 and 1543.[10] That is, the first ship arrived a year

---

10. Kishino Hisashi, *Seiōjin no Nihon hakken: Zabieru rainichizen Nihon jōhō no kenkyū* [Discovery of Japan by Western Europeans: Research on Information about Japan before Xavier's Arrival] (Tokyo: Yoshikawa Kōbunkan, 1989), 20, 26.

before the Portuguese introduced firearms on Tanegashima Island.

Valuable records left from these unexpected encounters exist because Ryukyuan people expanded their activities into Southeast Asia.

The End of a Glorious Era

In the sixteenth century, European powers represented by Portugal and Spain began to expand, and massive numbers of Chinese merchants ventured overseas once again as the Ming dynasty's authority weakened and it became unable to enforce the maritime travel ban. With these developments, Ryukyu's overseas trade went into decline. In addition, in the second half of the sixteenth century, after Japanese traders expanded directly into Southeast Asia, Ryukyu's Southeast Asian trade came to an end. Its great ships vanished from the records after the last visit to Siam in 1570. The East Asian and Southeast Asian world transformed into a vast sphere of private and civilian trading, and Ryukyu lost its position as a transit trade hub. With the decline of trade, Kumemura became a ghost town. Its Chinese residents left in search of other business opportunities, and those leaving Fujian to work overseas went to Southeast Asia instead of Kumemura.

It should be noted, however, that a small number of Chinese residents remained in Kumemura. In the seventeenth century their numbers increased through the settling of shipwrecked or stranded Chinese people there. Chinese-speaking Ryukyuans were also added to the Kumemura registry, leading to a revival of Kumemura in the early modern period.

Amid all these new changes, only the tribute trade with China and the Japan trade conducted via Japanese merchant traders remained. A glorious era came to a close as the history of Asia shifted with the tides of change.

CHAPTER III

3. In Search of Possible Ryukyuan History

Visiting Southeast Asia

I have often taken the opportunity to travel to places with a connection to Ryukyu's overseas trade. To close this chapter, I will recount some of my experiences.

My travels began in 1974 with a trip to Southeast Asia. I visited many ports where Ryukyuan ships had dropped anchor, such as Malacca, Ayutthaya, Sunda Kelapa (Jakarta), and Palembang, among others. My very first impression of Malacca was startling. There was zero trace of the city that had held such an advantageous position in the East-West trade that it became the center of trade in Southeast Asia. Nothing remained to convey the once magnificent history of the Malacca Sultanate, proud of the brilliant prosperity that had brought the Ryukyuan ships to visit every year.

If there is no evidence in Malacca to show a connection with Ryukyu, then we must work from within a reconsideration of the history of Ryukyu to build a historical narrative that can fill in the blanks. I have explored these thoughts further in my book *Ryūkyū no jidai* (The Age of Ryukyu) and have since revisited Malacca many times. With each visit, the Malaccan scenery presents me with new aspects of that historical narrative.

Experiences in Quanzhou

I was finally able to visit China in 1981. Although diplomatic relations between Japan and China had been restored before then, Fujian Province, where I wanted to visit, had been among the areas that remained closed to foreigners for a period of time. Since then, I have made several visits to Quanzhou and Fuzhou (both in Fujian), as well as Guangzhou (in Guangdong), Nanjing (Jiangsu), Beijing, and other places linked with Ryukyu. Quanzhou and Fuzhou were the entry ports for Ryukyuan ships; Guangzhou was a stopover for Ryukyuan ships bound for Southeast Asia. Nanjing was the capital of the early Ming dynasty, and the location of the Nanjing Guozijian (Nanjing National Central University), which was the highest institute of education and where many Ryukyuan exchange students went to study. And, of course, Beijing was the final destination for the tributary missions.

Until the time of the Yuan dynasty (1271–1368), Quanzhou, the designated port of entry for Ryukyu for the hundred-year period from 1372 to 1472, had been renowned as the largest trade port in China. Even Marco Polo made special note of its prosperity in *The Travels of Marco Polo*. On my first visit to Quanzhou, I organized a small informal meeting with guest researchers at the famous Quanzhou Maritime Museum. However, they ignored me to engage each other in a heated discussion over the question of why the Maritime Trade Office had moved from Quanzhou to Fuzhou in 1472. One person asserted, "The harbor had silted up and became unusable as a shipping port." Another rebutted, saying, "No, that's not it. There was rampant smuggling based out of Quanzhou, making it an unsuitable location for the Maritime Trade Office." I could only admire the intensity with which these Chinese researchers enjoyed their debate.

The *Chongwu suocheng zhi* (Chongwu City Annals) is a record of Chongwu village's history in which an account during the early Ming era states that the community leaders had gifted the Ryukyu Chūzan king a "four hundred-ryō battleship," possibly in response to an order from the Ming government. I was able to obtain a copy of this passage and it provided new evidence in support of the idea that the early Ming dynasty had allocated seafaring vessels to the Ryukyuans free of charge. In addition, I learned that in the Quanzhou area, the term *zuo Liuqiu* (lit. "work Ryukyu") used to refer to those who engaged in trade with Ryukyu. This term is noteworthy because it hints at the involvement of private and merchant traders, and their connection with Ryukyu.

Also in Quanzhou, a local researcher gave me access to a family registry, a Chinese genealogy called the *Qingyuan Lin Li zongzupu* (Qingyuan Lin Li Family Genealogical Record). The registry contains an article about Lin Yi An and his son serving as *tutongshi* responsible for the care of a tribute delegation that had come from Ryukyu. The term *tutongshi* refers to interpreters who spoke the Ryukyuan language. Their position served an important function in mediating between the Ryukyuans and the Maritime Trade Office.[11] Though many of the members in the Ryukyuan delegation spoke Chinese, there were still interpreters and caretakers involved. The Lins, father and son, were active in the 1460s, and I wondered how they had learned the Ryukyuan language. Did they learn it from Ryukyuans residing in Quanzhou? Or did they make frequent trips to Ryukyu via the private and merchant trade routes?

Traces of Exchanges with Ryukyu

It took me about four hours to drive north from Quanzhou to Fuzhou, the port designated exclusively for Ryukyu from 1472 until the collapse of the Ryukyu Kingdom in 1879. The Jū'en'eki (Fuzhou Ryukyu House) was established there. The location of the Ryukyu House can still be clearly identified, and in 1992, a memorial hall was

---

11. This position was later called *hekou tongshi* (lit. "river mouth interpreter").

built on the site. There are also several tombs in the city outskirts, dating from the early modern period, of Ryukyuans who died while in the area; these are marked and preserved as cultural assets of the city. Fuzhou is a city with many traces of exchanges with Ryukyu, filling me with a sense of tense excitement as I walked in the very places where the scenes of history had played out.

From Fuzhou I chartered a boat to take me down the Min River and visit the Wuhumen, the "Gate of Five Tigers" that lies across the mouth of the river and served as the entry and exit point for the tribute ships, all the while comparing the physical locations to the Ryukyuan records. In addition, with the cooperation of researchers from Fujian, I explored the villages that were once home to those

Ryukyuan grave in Fuzhou. The grave of Genka Ufunjō (Chinese name, Xiang Weifan), a Ryukyuan engaged in the tribute trade who died of illness in Fuzhou in 1718. Photo by Takara Kurayoshi.

CHAPTER III

who would become Kumemura residents, emigrating to Ryukyu in order to support the overseas trade. Through all of these investigations, I made many new discoveries. Then, departing from Fuzhou and starting for distant Beijing, I relied on the records of my predecessors to navigate through the most challenging obstacle on the Ryukyuan tribute delegations' journey, the Xianxia mountain range on the border between Fujian and Zhejiang.

I continue to travel to places with connections to Ryukyu's overseas trade. There are many points that I wish to confirm from the Ryukyuan historical perspective, and at the same time, my purpose is to understand the circumstances that cannot be known just from this perspective alone.

Still, my true purpose is to experience the spatial extent and depth of ancient Ryukyu. Instead of viewing the history of Ryukyu as merely the regional history of a small island society or enclosing its history into the narrow confines of conventional "Japanese history" or "local history," I needed to experience the historical spaces in which Ryukyuan history itself unfolded. To do so, I needed to physically experience being in the actual places in Asia connected to Ryukyu. I wanted to internalize *Ryukyu in Asia* not as a theory, but as the conscious realm of a historian.

With world history's "Age of Discovery" in mind, I call the period from the end of the fourteenth century to the mid-sixteenth century, when Ryukyu's flourishing overseas trade stretched across the Asian world, "The Age of Great Trade." Why does this period, overlapping with the era of ancient Ryukyu, need its own distinct label? There are two reasons for this. The first is that we must understand the processes that shaped the kingdom of ancient Ryukyu in the context of the wider Asian world, so I wished to emphasize the Asian historical characteristics visible in ancient Ryukyu. The second reason, and connected with the first, is to highlight how the benefits of trade became the material foundation of the kingdom, and how its interactions with the international community played the role of teacher as the kingdom took shape.

Just as the specific historical developments of ancient Ryukyu suggest, the study of Ryukyuan history must also always be approached with the Asian world in mind. Believing such a flexible awareness of spatial context indispensable to an understanding of Ryukyuan history, I proposed the concept of "The Age of Great Trade."

CHAPTER IV
THE KINGDOM OF WRITS

CHAPTER IV

1. Rediscovery

A Look at the Royal Government System

As shown in the previous chapter, after that first visit to Malacca, I continued to visit the locations where the Ryukyuan trade ships made port. Through these efforts, I was able to confirm Ryukyu's historical reach, and to see the kingdom's position in the increasingly international world spanning from East Asia to Southeast Asia. However, when the time came to return home, I always suffered feelings of frustration as I settled my tired body into the airplane seat. Yet again, a fresh historical narrative had failed to emerge—some crucial details were missing—and the more I grasped the breadth of the picture as a whole, the stronger my frustration grew.

In fact, the source of my frustration was easy to identify. I kept imagining those Ryukyuans boarding their ships and sailing across the rough seas to carry out their duties, yet the details surrounding them prior to setting sail remained a mystery. What kinds of organizations did they belong to? What kinds of work did they perform, and how? In short, I did not know anything about their work while ashore.

The job of managing Ryukyu's overseas trade was performed on behalf of the king by the king's staff. What were the staff's onshore duties and, by extension, what kind of organizational structure did they belong to as public officials? What organization, bearing resemblance to that of a trading company, directed the overseas trade? These questions needed clarification. Given that the overseas trade was publicly managed, clarifying the details of this "trading company" would be the same as elucidating the administrative structure of the

THE KINGDOM OF WRITS

Ryukyu Kingdom itself. I already knew that the services performed by the residents of Kumemura made them indispensable to the overseas trade. However, I needed an understanding of the central entity employing the Kumemura residents, the same royal government administrative structure directing the overseas trade: the Shuri royal government system.

With the matter in need of clarification crystal clear, what next? The historical records are almost completely nonexistent. On the Ryukyuan side, historical documents from the ancient Ryukyu era, limited to the diplomatic communications recorded in the *Rekidai hōan* and the religious songs collected in the *Omoro sōshi*, do not provide much insight into the functions of the royal government. Finally, even with the growing successes of archaeological excavations, newly discovered structures and artifacts don't shed any light on the situation. The royal government's administrative system was, of course, not literally buried underground. Faced with these undeniable facts, I resigned myself to the non-existence of any historical documents. Then I met Mr. Araki Moriaki.

"Historical documents are like musical instruments"

In 1976, Mr. Araki had left the University of Tokyo's Institute of Social Science and was by then working as a professor at Okinawa University, engaged in reevaluating Ryukyuan historical research from the ground up. I had frequent opportunities to encounter his keen wit, whether on methods of analyzing historical documents, or on the logical construction of historical narratives, and I was often both humbled and inspired by his sharp insights. One day we were sitting in a snack bar drinking beer, when Mr. Araki said, "I think historical documents are like musical instruments. First, you need the skills to play the instrument. Then, as a performer, you have to draw out the best music that instrument can produce."

Historical documents as musical instruments, to be played by the historian as a skilled performer—these two phrases were the keys that opened my eyes. I had a sense of what Mr. Araki basically meant. He was referring to the potential held by the writs of appointment. Even before this, Mr. Araki would emphasize their importance in the study of ancient Ryukyu to the researchers around him whenever he had the opportunity. I had heard him say several times, "We can get a clear view of ancient Ryukyu with the writs as our lens." I felt he was pressing sharply for us to re-examine them, not with common sense, but by taking a more rigorous approach and treating them like musical instruments that needed great skill to bring out their full potential.

A writ of appointment (J. *jireisho*, Ch. *cilingshu*) was essentially an order, an official statement of public appointment much like the letters of appointment still in wide use today. It is no exaggeration to say that upon hearing Mr. Araki's expert advice that evening, I was inspired to use the writs of appointment, still extant in many locations, to explore the inner workings of the royal government of the Ryukyu Kingdom during its encounter with the Asian world.

Archival Research Begins

A few days later, I set out, accompanied by Mr. Araki, to examine some historical documents. I had heard that there was a family in the town of Motobu in the north of Okinawa Island with some old papers that could possibly be writs of appointment. We were joined by my colleague, Mr. Nakachi Tetsuo from Okinawa International University, and the three of us went to find out what exactly these papers were.

We arrived in the Henachi neighborhood of Motobu to visit the

Nakamura family, known for having produced generations of *noro* (publicly appointed local priestesses). Our host took down a frame hanging above the family altar and opened it to show us three old documents, wrinkled with age.

They were definitely writs of appointment. Smoothing out the wrinkles with great care, we found one from the 32nd year of the Wanli era (1604) appointing a Henachi *mezashi* (a local public official); another from Wanli 35 appointed a woman named Makatō as the Gushikawa *noro*; and a third from Wanli 40 appointed a Jahana *okite* (another local public office). They were about 30 centimeters tall and 40 centimeters wide, written in an elegant, cursive hiragana script. At the top, 10-centimeter square vermilion ink seals reading *"Shuri no in"* were stamped in both the left and right corners.

Of course, this was not the first time I had seen writs of appointment. For example, I had seen the thirty-two writs of appointment handed down in the Dana family of Shuri. The strange thing was that when I had no particular interest in them, they were just part of the background scenery, and didn't leave any strong impression. However, the three writs in Henachi seemed fresh, and they shone with a compelling aura. To borrow Mr. Araki's words, they were instruments I was eager to play.

Since that day, I have made an exhaustive search for information about the writs of appointment, organizing my findings into files. The conditions of the extant writs vary greatly. In some cases, the originals have been beautifully preserved; in others, only photographs of the originals remain. Some I found only because they were included in another document, or an earlier researcher had copied them into a notebook; other times, printed materials included incomplete writs. Seventeen years have passed since we saw those originals that day in Henachi, Motobu, and in that time, with the help of many different people, I have been able to identify more than two hundred writs of appointment.

CHAPTER IV

Accordingly, I have become immersed in this research project, of trying to see what music I can produce from these documents, on the theme of the Ryukyu Kingdom's royal government administrative system.

2. What Is Reflected?

Reading the Henachi Writs of Appointment

Make note of the dates mentioned in each of the Henachi writs. The recorded dates are given according to the Chinese imperial era. When converted to the Western calendar, they range from 1604 to 1612. During this period, the Ryukyu Kingdom struggled with the oppressive demands made by Tokugawa Ieyasu and the Shimazu clan in Satsuma until finally, an invasion by a Satsuma military force of three thousand soldiers in the spring of 1609 brought the kingdom under military occupation. This was a time of literally unprecedented national crisis.

The three writs of appointment from Henachi show that the administrative task of creating them and appointing personnel continued even during such turbulent circumstances, and the tradition of accepting sought-after positions as *noro* or local officials continued intact. I couldn't help but wonder at the stately calm emanating from their words, as if there was no crisis unfurling.

Obviously, writs of appointment are official documents used to appoint people to specific positions. Furthermore, these documents are used on a single occasion to make the appointment. It follows that they carry a specific date, and outlandish motives notwithstanding, there is no reason later generations would create forgeries of such documents.

Working from the principle that the dates on the writs reflect the true dates of their creation, the fact that the three from Henachi date from the period around the Shimazu Invasion establishes beyond a doubt that the appointment process continued despite the upheaval. They might seem to present a debatable scenario: in this period of national crisis and military occupation by Satsuma forces, the impact of their control did not substantially change daily life in Ryukyu.

However, this is not the case. The Henachi writs show that the invasion and conquest by Satsuma's military forces did, of course, have a profound impact on Ryukyu. Tedious as it may be, I will illustrate this point by quoting from two of the writs of appointment.

A: Gushikawa *noro* writ of appointment (1607)

Shiyo[ri] no [omikoto]
[stamp] Miyakizen magiri no
 Gushikawa noro mata chi tomo ni
 Gojū nuki chi hatake yon ohoso
 Gushikawa haru mata Niyohabaru mata Hamakawa haru
 mata Hoki haru tomo ni
 Moto no noro no kuwa
 Hitori Makatō ni
[stamp] Tamawari mōshi sōrō
Shiyori yori Makatō ga hō he mairu
Manreki sanjūgo nen shichi gatsu jūgo nichi

Writ of Shuri
The Nakijin district
Gushikawa *noro* with properties
Fifty *nuki* of arable land, in total four
Gushikawa field, also Niyoha field, also Hamakawa field, also Hoki field, inclusive
To the previous *noro*'s heir

CHAPTER IV

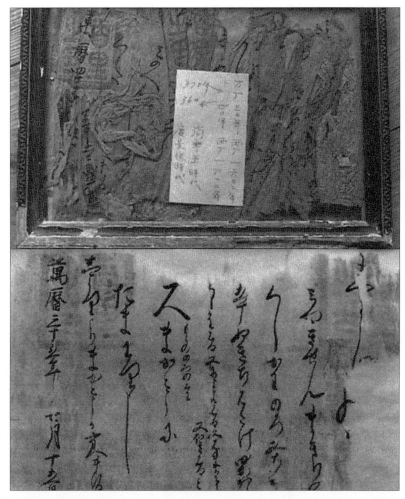

Henachi Nakamura family writ of appointment. Condition at the time of discovery (top). Enclosed in a frame, it was unclear how many documents were included. The Gushikawa *noro*'s writ of appointment after restoration (bottom). This is the writ referred to as "A" in this text. Photos by Takara Kurayoshi.

One Makatō
Hereby ordered.
From Shuri to Makatō delivered
Wanli 35th year, 7th month, 15th day

Touching only on the main points, this document appoints Makatō, daughter of the previous incumbent, as the Gushikawa *noro* in Nakijin *magiri*, and bestows the rights to fifty *nuki* of arable land as a source of income. A *magiri* (O. *majiri*) is an administrative district, and a *nuki* is an area measurement; more on this in Chapter 5. The word Shiyori (Shuri) at the beginning refers to the king.

The second writ of appointment has not been preserved in as good condition, but it reads as follows:

B: Jahana *okite* writ of appointment (1612)

Shiyori no omikoto
[stamp] Miyakizen magiri no
  Jiyahana no oki [te ha]
  Mi no heban no [missing]
  [Missing. Obviously included "hitori" in the beginning as in the previous example]
[stamp] kudasare sōrō
Manreki yonjū nen jūni gatsu hachi [nichi]

Writ of Shuri
The Nakijin district
Jahana *okite*
Guard of the Snake (missing)
(Missing. Probably included "To one [name]")
Order sent down
Wanli 40th year, 12th month, 8th day

CHAPTER IV

Here, a man (unfortunately, the name is missing, but the position was typically held by a man) is being appointed to the administrative office of *okite* in Jahana, Nakijin district. Jahana is a *shima* (subdistrict) of Nakijin, and the official in charge of a *shima* was called the *okite*.

The two documents are only five years apart, with A made in 1607, and B in 1612. Despite this, in comparing the two, we can see that the line in A, *"Shiyori yori Makatō ga hō he mairu"* (From Shuri to Makatō delivered) is completely missing from B. Upon examination of other writs of appointment, those from the same period as B and later all lack a line corresponding to that one. It is clear that the invasion and conquest by Satsuma in 1609 resulted in a change in the phrasing of these official documents.

Ever since I first saw these writs of appointment in Henachi, I have often pondered why such changes came about. The sentence stipulating that in the name of Shiyori (Shuri, i.e., the king), this writ of appointment grants a post to a specific person, Makatō, is an important one. Perhaps its disappearance signifies a weakening of the king's authority under Satsuma's rule. But this cannot be the case, since the phrase *Shiyori no omikoto*, where *Shiyori* refers to the king and *omikoto* refers to a royal writ, appears in both A and B. Unfortunately, I have yet to find the key to solve this mystery.

Why did the phrase, *"Shiyori yori Makatō ga hō he mairu"* (From Shuri to Makatō delivered) disappear? As I stubbornly and repeatedly struggled with this question, I again recalled Mr. Araki's words. I realized I needed to completely rethink my approach in order to reveal the "best music" that these documents could produce. Obsessing over why a single line had disappeared was no way to produce the "best music."

In order to hear the "best music," I needed to go back to the basics in my thinking of the writs of appointment. I began my research, accordingly, with the decision that rather than dissecting each one in a scattered manner, my fundamental approach would be to start by understanding and prioritizing the overall form, while still valuing the interpretation of each character and phrase.

The Principles of a Letter of Appointment

What are the characteristics of official documents like writs of appointment (issued by the royal government) or modern-day letters of appointment (issued by a company)? Let's begin by reviewing the basic characteristics of letters of appointment and other official employment documents.

A letter of appointment necessarily presupposes the existence of a specific organization or group. If we refer to the entity with the authority to grant an appointment as the "issuer," and the entity receiving it as the "recipient," both names must be clearly stated in the document. This is necessary to identify the issuer, who specifies the recipient and issues the letter of appointment. Next, the issuer must specify what is being granted to the recipient, stating explicitly the purpose in issuing the document. This gives concrete information, such as appointing someone to be a facility director, or naming a director of sales. I call this the "salary details." Another important piece of information must specify when the letter goes into effect, that is, the formal start date of the appointment. Let's call this the "date of issuance."

In other words, a letter of appointment has four essential components: the issuer, the recipient, position and salary details, and a date of issuance. To put it simply, it is a formal document that makes clear when, under whose authority, for whom, and what is being granted.

Let's reconsider the previous writs of appointment, A and B. In A, the issuer was "Shiyori" (i.e., Shuri, the king); the recipient was a woman, Makatō. The appointment granted her the position of Gushikawa *noro* in the Nakijin district, and also provided a source of

CHAPTER IV

income in the form of a 50-*nuki* grant of arable land. The date of issuance was on the fifteenth day of the seventh month of Wanli 35 (1607). For B, the issuer was the same "Shiyori," but the recipient's identity is unclear although it was certainly a man. The position granted was as a local official, the Jahana *okite*, and date of issuance was on the eighth day of the twelfth month of Wanli 40 (1612). Clearly, both writs completely satisfy the structural elements of such documents.

So, what exactly is the purpose of a letter of appointment in the first place?

As previously mentioned, a letter of appointment assumes the existence of a specific organization or group. Further, such a letter is used exclusively within the organization or group, and never intended for external use. The relationship between the issuer and the recipient is an organizational one existing within the structure of an institution, and in no way expresses a personal or private relationship. In the impersonal logic of an organization, even if the company president and the head of sales go to a bar after work to socialize as friends over drinks, their relationship remains strictly within the confines of their organization, as expressed by a letter of appointment. On the premise of such structural relationships, the president has the authority to appoint the head of sales to that position, and to ensure the effectiveness of that appointment. In turn, they are responsible for fulfilling the duties laid out by the president. The very existence of an organization or group is based on these kinds of internal structural relationships.

Let's say that for some reason, a company known as "The Ryukyu Kingdom, Inc." disappears. Supposing that all the documents with the company's profile and organizational chart are missing, how would we be able to comprehend its internal organization?

In my case, I would visit the homes of people who had previously worked for the company and photograph any documents they might have stored there, such as any letters of appointment mentioning the company president. In doing so, I could collect a variety of job titles, including chairman, vice chairman, president, executive director, managing director, director of sales, general affairs manager, chief of maintenance and repair, the assistant director of customer service, the section chief, and so on. Arranging these titles in their relative positions within the organization and scrutinizing their pecking order might reveal a somewhat hazy but suggestive picture of the internal structure of "The Ryukyu Kingdom, Inc."

In short, letters of appointment mirror the internal dynamics of an organization or group. Of course, a single letter reflects only a single point, but we can begin to grasp the overall picture by connecting the dots gleaned from a large collection of such letters.

Reframing my approach in using the writs of appointment to illustrate the internal organization of the Ryukyu Kingdom, specifically to sketch an image of the Shuri royal government, brought me to my task of examining each document individually for the dots it could provide. And with those dots, I could then identify the lines that connect them.

3. What the Document Format Reveals

Three Types of Writ

The first task I tackled was the issue of the format and changes in the writs of appointment.

Of the 202 writs I had collected, the oldest dated from 1523, and the most recent from 1874, a time span of 350 years. The one from 1523 had been written during the reign of King Shō Shin (r. 1477–1526), introduced in Chapter 2, the king who led the Ryukyu Kingdom to its greatest heights. King Shō Tai (r. 1848–79), the last king, was on the

CHAPTER IV

throne when the most recent writ was issued in 1874. Five years later, in 1879, the kingdom itself vanished with the annexation of Ryukyu and the establishment of Okinawa Prefecture.

Due to the length of this time period, I refer to the 202 writs of appointment collectively as the "Ryukyuan writs." I arranged them in chronological order and conducted a detailed and comprehensive examination of their formats and changes over time. As a result, it became clear that the Ryukyuan writs could be grouped into three types based on format.

The first type, exemplified by writ A, was written entirely in hiragana, and without exception

King Shō Tai (1843–1901). Reproduced from Higashionna Kanjun, *Shō Tai kō jitsuroku* (True Account of Marquess Shō Tai), 1924. Courtesy of Naha City Museum of History.

contained an addressee line corresponding to *"From Shuri to Makatō delivered."* The second type, like writ B, lacks that line, and as time progresses, shows an increasing number of Chinese characters included with the hiragana. The third type is written entirely in Chinese characters.

It is worth noting how the three types line up neatly along the timeline. The first type appears first, followed by the second after the Shimazu Invasion of 1609, and the third was in use from 1667 until the kingdom was abolished. In other words, the three types of writs transitioned successively from one to the next, representing different stages in chronological order; for this I named them the "ancient Ryukyu set," "transition period set," and "early modern Ryukyu set." Accordingly, if I happened to find a writ of appointment lacking a date, it was a simple matter to determine a general date for it based on its format.

There is much to consider in answering the question of why the Shimazu Invasion triggered the change from the ancient Ryukyu style to that of the transition period, but we do know the reason for the change to the early modern style in 1667. In the early modern period, the kingdom underwent a period of reconstruction led by the political figure Shō Shōken (also known as Haneji Chōshū).[1] His comprehensive administrative reforms led to significant revisions in the existing system, including a reduction in the number of appointments by writ.

Through this work, it has become apparent to me that the writs of appointment are deeply connected to the changes that occurred in the Ryukyu Kingdom; that is to say, those changes seem to be reflected in the writs. In addition, through these documents we can gain insight into the royal administrative system of the Ryukyu Kingdom. Those dating from ancient Ryukyu, for example, provide concrete data to explore the period in which the kingdom reached across Asia. Here it is important to note that because the writs of appointment came into use during the reign of Shō Shin, they do not extend back to earlier periods like the Sanzan era or the First Shō dynasty. Thus, the ancient Ryukyu set does not cover the entire period, due to the limitation of the historical documents themselves.

Currently, my collection of verified writs of appointment consists of 58 writs from ancient Ryukyu, 35 from the transitional period, and 109 from the early modern period. The ancient Ryukyu set represents only about 29 percent of the total. With the passage of more than four hundred years, there are only a few that remain from that period.

---

1. Shō Shōken (1617–75), a member of the royal family, also wrote *Chūzan seikan* (Mirror of Chūzan), the first book on the history of the Ryukyu Kingdom.

CHAPTER IV

By sorting the ancient Ryukyu set of 58 according to the recipients' locations, we find that 26 are from Amami district, 31 are from Okinawa district (Okinawa Island and neighboring islands), and one is from Sakishima district (the Miyako and Yaeyama groups). A similar list for the transition period set reveals 29 from Okinawa and six from Sakishima. For the early modern set, Okinawa has 86, and Sakishima 23. In other words, after the ancient Ryukyu period, no writs of appointment were issued for Amami district. The reason for this is simple. Until the Shimazu Invasion of 1609, the Amami district had been a part of the Ryukyu Kingdom's territories; after the invasion and conquest, however, it was ceded and came under the direct rule of the Satsuma domain.

The distribution of the writs of appointment clearly represents the territorial extent of the Ryukyu Kingdom. Therefore, the concept of "Ryukyu," which encompassed the three districts—Amami, Okinawa, and Sakishima—must be understood to include Amami when studying the ancient Ryukyu set of writs of appointment.

Rejecting the Hereditary System

The logic of the writs of appointment is based on the rejection of a hereditary system. For example, if Mr. Suzuki, the director of sales, were transferred to another position and his eldest son automatically stepped into that position, then there would be no need for a writ of appointment.

In example A of the Henachi writs, when the woman who had previously been the Gushikawa *noro* perhaps died or retired due to illness, there was no reason to assume her daughter Makatō would automatically succeed her. If any suitable candidates beside Makatō were available, they would also have had a chance to become the Gushikawa *noro*.

In practice, the position may have passed from mother to daughter, but Makatō could be recognized as the Gushikawa *noro* only once she had received the writ of appointment bearing the king's seal. To repeat, Makatō became *noro*, not because she was the daughter and heir of the previous *noro*, but because of her official appointment to the post through a writ of appointment from the king.

However, a closer look at the extant writs related to *noro* appointments reveals that successors were limited to relatives within the third degree of kinship: the baton passed from mother to daughter, grandmother to granddaughter, older sister to younger, or aunt to niece. Apparently, positions such as *noro* were passed down within certain bloodlines.

Noro priestesses were found in the various regions serving as public religious functionaries and presiding over community religious rituals. In particular, they played an important role in leading their local community in the national-level agricultural rituals. The official nature of their position is reflected in the fact that they were formally appointed through writs, and in the case of Makatō in writ A, by the fact that she was granted farmland as a source of income. When a *noro* position was vacated, the local community would send a type of petition to the royal government in Shuri to suggest a suitable successor. The royal government would create a new writ of appointment with the king's seal naming the recommended woman as the new *noro*.

The essential point here is that though the issuing authority respected the community's desire to grant the position of *noro* to Makatō, it was the Shuri royal government that ultimately had the authority to grant the appointment. Even while respecting the collective will of the local community, according to the royal government's logic, royal authorization was necessary and required a writ of appointment to convey that official endorsement. In some areas, a *noro* was referred to as "*Goshuin Ganashi*," wherein *ganashi* is a poetic suffix of respect and *goshuin* refers to the "*Shuri no in*," the seal of Shuri stamped on the writ. By extension, *goshuin* became an alternative term for writs of appointment. This usage, meaning, in effect, "Lady Writ," symbolized the invocation of the king's authority beyond the community's collective will.

If the system of hereditary office was rejected and a writ of appointment was issued every time a new *noro* was handed the baton in the transfer of office, then there must have been a corresponding number of writs created. The *Ryūkyū-koku yuraiki* (Records of the Origins of the Country of Ryukyu, 1713)[2] reports that at the beginning of the eighteenth century, there were at least two hundred women serving as *noro* in the Okinawa district (Okinawa Island and its surrounding islands). Based on this figure, and assuming an average tenure of thirty years in office, this implies that in the one hundred years of the sixteenth century, for example, there should have been more than 660 writs of appointment issued.

The Supposed Vast Number of Writs

Among the set of extant writs dating from ancient Ryukyu, only eight are related to the appointment of a *noro*: barely the tip of the iceberg. The one appointing Makatō's mother did not survive. We must count ourselves fortunate to have the daughter's.

The system was not limited to female religious functionaries like the *noro* but was applied equally to male officials as well. Consider the following:

---

2. Compiled by the Shuri royal government, the *Ryūkyū-koku yuraiki* is a topography of ancient Ryukyu. The text describes official functions and the government post system at Shuri in addition to the origins and records of ancient customs found throughout the kingdom.

C: Ushuku *Ōyako* Writ of Appointment (1529)
   Shiyori no o[mi]koto
   [stamp] Kasari magiri no
      Usuku no ōyako ha
      Moto no Shiyori no ōyako ga kuwa
      Hitori Chiyakumoi ni
   [stamp] Tamawari mōshi [sōrō]
   [Shiyori yori Chiyakumoi ga hō he mairu]
   Kasei hachi nen jūni gatsu nijūku nichi

Writ of Shuri
The Kasari district
Ushuku *ōyako*
To the previous Shuri *ōyako*'s son
One Chiyakumoi
Hereby ordered
(From Shuri to Chiyakumoi delivered)
Kasei 8th year, 12th month, 29th day

Ushuku was a subdistrict within Kasari *magiri*, a district in Amami Ōshima. The local administrative official of the subdistrict was known as Ushuku *ōyako*. The father of Chiyakumoi, named in the writ, had served as Shuri *ōyako* (another local official), and had retired (since the writ refers to the "previous Shuri *ōyako*"). Now, Chiyakumoi had the good fortune to be appointed to the position of Ushuku *ōyako*. Chiyakumoi's father had likely also received a writ of appointment as Shuri *ōyako*. Again, the son's letter has been preserved, but the father's has been lost to time.

   In the Ryukyu Kingdom, every public official appointed to office, whether male or female, was appointed by a writ. Therefore, it is reasonable to assume that the number of appointment letters that once existed must have corresponded to the number of appointments made to public office.

Not only that, but just as is the case today, a system of personnel transfers was needed for officials, and the following is an example of how the Ryukyu Kingdom was no exception to this:

D: Na'on *Okite* Writ of Transfer (1556)

> *Shiyori no omikoto*
> *[stamp] Yakeuchi magiri no*
>   *Nagara no okite ha*
>   *Hitori Na'on no okite ni*
> *[stamp] Tamawari mōshi sōrō*
> *Shiyori yori Na'on no okite no hō he mairu*
> *Kasei sanjūgo nen hachi gatsu jūichi nichi*

> Writ of Shuri
> Yakeuchi district[3]
> Nagara *okite*
> To one Na'on *okite*
> Hereby ordered
> From Shuri to Na'on *okite* delivered
> Kasei 35th year, 8th month, 11th day

Here, an individual who had been serving as the *okite* of Na'on in the Yakiuchi district of Amami Ōshima is being transferred to the position of *okite* in Nagara in the same district. There are many examples of this type of transfer writ, with some cases being transfers to equivalent

---

3. Modern Yakiuchi district. *Ke* and *ki* were both pronounced ki in many dialects, as reflected by the discrepancy here.

positions like this one, and other cases known to be promotions to a higher-ranking office.

Since writs of appointment were issued for each transfer, we can stipulate that the original number of writs would have been the sum of the number of appointments and transfers. This presumably enormous number gives rise to the fitting description of the Ryukyu Kingdom as the "Kingdom of Writs."

CHAPTER V
THE ORGANIZATION OF THE KINGDOM

CHAPTER V

1. Various Officials

The Elite Class:
The Royal Family and Central Government Officials

If the fifty-eight writs of appointment from ancient Ryukyu are the messengers reporting on the circumstances of the one-time "Kingdom of Writs," then we must use the information recorded in them to uncover the real state of affairs in the Ryukyu Kingdom. Let's attempt a brief description of the picture that emerges from these writs, with assistance from historical materials created during the early modern period, such as official histories, different types of chronicles, inscriptions, and so on. First and foremost, we can learn the contemporary names of the positions and rankings from the writs. What were these positions, and how were they organized?

As previously described, the king, at the apex of the kingdom's internal organization, had the authority to appoint officials and priestesses to various positions. The king himself was known by a variety of titles: *ōyo no nushi* (lord of the great world), *yo no nushi* (lord of the world), *ushuganashi* (honorable lord), *teda* (the sun), and *Shiyori* (Shuri). The term *yo* (world) referred to Ryukyu in its entirety, so *ōyo no nushi* and *yo no nushi* became alternative titles for the king in the meaning of sovereign. As indicated earlier, the meaning of *ushu* in *ushuganashi* is "honorable lord" with *ganashi* being a poetic suffix of respect. *Teda* means "the sun" and there are many examples of religious songs portraying the king as the sun on earth with the imagery of the sun symbolizing the great king. *Shiyori* is Shuri, the royal capital and synonymous with Shuri Castle, and by extension this became another alternative title for the king. The king, both as the authority issuing writs of appointment and holder of a hereditary position, was obviously never named as the recipient of a writ of appointment. He was only ever the issuer, and without exception, he is referred to as *Shiyori* in the writs.

How do ranks appear in titles for the royal family? According to inscriptions and other sources, key figures in the king's family, including the queen or courtesans, princes and princesses, siblings, and other relatives, appear to have held the title of *aji*. For example, in King Shō Shin's case, his mother was referred to as the *ōaji* (great *aji*) of Yosoe Udun; his daughter was the *aji* of Sasukasa; his five sons were the *aji* of Nakagusuku, Nakijin, Goeku, Kin, and Tomigusuku.[1] Until the fifteenth century, *aji* had referred to the ruling class that held strong regional ties and were based around the local *gusuku*. However, as a result of their permanent relocation to Shuri under King Shō Shin's policy, the title of *aji* underwent a transformation to become a designation for elite members of the royal family.

There is also the term *anjibe* or *ajibe*. The character for *be* indicates a hierarchical level or class. It refers to a group within the hierarchy claiming the title of *aji*, associated with elite members of the royal family. Another term, *omoiguwabe*, serves as a collective term for princes and princesses. *Omoi* is an honorific prefix, and *guwa* means "child." The establishment of these usages show an awareness that the royal family was a distinct class, and further, that this idea had become institutionalized.

Among the officials serving the king, there was a distinction between those in the central and local governments. Central officials, residing in the kingdom's nexus formed by the political center at Shuri

---

1. Inscription in the Tama-udun Mausoleum, 1501.

and the commercial and trading center of Naha, were elite officials. In particular, the royal capital that formed around Shuri Castle was known as Shuri Oyaguni with *oya* (parent) being an honorific prefix for *kuni* (country), highlighting its position as the kingdom's center.

In the writs of appointment, central officials were titled *ōyakomoi*. While *-moi* is an honorific suffix, unfortunately, the etymology of *ōyakomoi* remains unclear. Specifically, the district or subdistrict of an official's appointment would be included in the title. A person holding an appointment in the district of Urasoe, for example, would be titled *Urasoe no ōyakomoi*, or a person appointed to Urasoe's central subdistrict of Gusukuma would be *Gusukuma no ōyakomoi*, and so on. Over time, *ōyakomoi* was replaced by characters that could be read as *oyakumoi* (親雲上), but for some reason came to be pronounced as *pēchin*.

Those with the title of *ōyakomoi* included those who worked under the senior officials of the Yo'asutabe.[2] This *yo* uses the same Chinese character as the *yo* (world) in the titles *ōyo no nushi* and *yo no nushi*, which refer to the king; *asu* means elders; *ta* is a plural marker; and *be* is a group in a hierarchy. Taken together, the term can be understood to designate a group of elders in Ryukyuan society. This group provided the ministers, who, in a group of three, supported the king. The *ōyakomoi* class included other temporary administrative titles, such as *sōbugyō* (general magistrate) and *ishibugyō* (stone magistrate).[3] At present, however, the titles of various magistrates and the term Yo'asutabe appear only in inscriptions and are not found in any known writ of appointment dating from the ancient Ryukyu period.

In sum, the king was advised by an elite class of bureaucrats residing in Shuri and Naha.

---

2. Sanshikan (Council of Three) in Sino-Japanese.
3. The stone magistrate oversaw the stonework of a castle, hence the name.

Local Government: The Magiri-Shima System

The term "local" refers to the entire territory of the kingdom outside of Shuri and Naha. There were a variety of titles for local government officials, but these personnel were organized based on the local-level administrative system called the *magiri-shima* system; *magiri* (district) and *shima* (subdistrict, lit. "island").

Shima referred to an administrative unit composed of one or more natural settlement groups, similar to the *mura* (villages) of the early modern era or the *aza* (local districts) of today. *Magiri*, the antecedent of the modern divisions of cities, towns, and villages were larger administrative regions encompassing multiple *shima*. The Henachi writs of appointment (A and B) discussed in the previous chapter contain references to *magiri*, Miyakizen (Nakijin), and *shima*, Gushikawa and Jahana. The writs from Amami (C and D) mention Kasari *magiri* and Yakeuchi *magiri*; Usuku, Nagara, and Na'on were *shima* names. Local areas and smaller islands were sorted into many *magiri* and *shima*, and this administrative system applied throughout the regions of Amami, Okinawa, and Sakishima. Government officials were appointed based on the *magiri-shima* system.

To begin, the position responsible for overseeing the administration of a district (*magiri*) was the Shuri ōyako. Writ C from the previous chapter names the father of Chiyakumoi, whom the writ appointed as the Usuku ōyako, as the former Shuri ōyako, implying that he had for some reason left his position (in this case, as the Kasari Shuri ōyako). The number of Shuri ōyako positions reflected the number of districts, and to distinguish between them, they had the district names included in the beginning of the titles, such as Nakijin Shuri ōyako, Kasari Shuri ōyako, Yakeuchi Shuri ōyako, and so on.

There also appears to have been an ōokite (great *okite*) position that played a role in district administration and assisted the Shuri ōyako.

CHAPTER V

Figure 6. **Diagram of Administrative Districts of Ancient Ryukyu (Okinawa Island)**

Schematic drawing based on the *Ryūkyū-koku takakiwa mechō* (Complete Register of the Country of Ryukyu). Okinawa Island was divided into twenty-eight greater administrative districts (*magiri*), including the special district of Shuri. Districts in the southern area were especially dense.

THE ORGANIZATION OF THE KINGDOM

Various officials were posted in each subdistrict (*shima*) making up a district, with titles *ōyako*, *yohito* (later pronounced *yunchu* in Okinawan), *okite*, and *mezashi*. All of them had the name of their subdistrict as a prefix in their title, as in XX *ōyako*, or YY *yunchu*, and so on. While those responsible for the administrative duties of a subdistrict were at the base-level of the system, they were also involved at the district level. The Jahana *okite*, Usuku *ōyako*, and Nagara *okite* that appear in the writs of appointment in the previous chapter are examples of subdistrict officials.

Notably, among these, the position of local *ōyako* seems to have been equivalent to that of Shuri *ōyako*. This is because, although this title included the name of the subdistrict, their primary duties were at the district level. In addition, among the writs from ancient Ryukyu, there are cases of an *ōyako* being transferred to work as a Shuri *ōyako* and other cases demonstrating the opposite. My immediate thought was that these transfers indicated a promotion or demotion. But, in fact, it appears that transfers from Shuri *ōyako* to local *ōyako* were common occurrences, not special measures. If personnel were routinely transferred between the two posts, then based on the principle of the writs of appointment, we can conclude that the two positions were of equal status.

All of the official positions discussed here were filled by members of the local elite and were not posts created as residential positions for persons dispatched from the Shuri royal government. In other words, the system was entirely based on employing local talent. The surviving writs of appointment passed down through the generations confirm this.

CHAPTER V

A Variety of Local Officials

A closer look at the placements of local government officials reveals a number of situations.

Shuri *ōyako* were established in all three regions of Amami, Okinawa, and Sakishima. But Sakishima differed in that the number of Shuri *ōyako* posted there did not match the number of districts. Furthermore, there was a special position of "great Shuri *ōyako*" that was senior to the other Shuri *ōyako*. In the early modern period, the great Shuri *ōyako* came to be called by the title of *kashira* (lit. "head") and referred to the senior official of the three-person Kuramoto, a branch office of the royal government that directly governed over Sakishima.

There are few historical records regarding the rank of *ōokite* (great *okite*), leaving the details of that role unclear. *Okite* were established in Amami and Okinawa, but not in Sakishima. *Ōyako* too, were only in Amami and Okinawa, but not in Sakishima. The lack of the rank of *ōyako*, which was likely equal to the Shuri *ōyako* within the district-level government, is probably explained by the special role created for the great Shuri *ōyako* in Sakishima. The position of *yojin*, or *yonin*, as well, were found only in Amami and Sakishima. *Mezashi* were found throughout all of Okinawa in addition to Amami and Sakishima, but a closer look at the Okinawa group shows that they were only in the northern part of Okinawa Island and its small neighboring islands, and none in the central or southern areas.

Organizational differences aside, the main point is that the *magiri-shima* system was implemented across the entire kingdom and the corresponding local officials were evenly distributed in their postings. Given the rejection of the hereditary system and the fact that these posts were subject to personnel transfers, these official positions were filled exclusively through the issuance of writs of appointment.

Thus, in the case of local officials, the writs of appointment symbolized the organizational relationship between them and the king: the king controlling the *magiri-shima* system and the local officials doing the administrative work within it. Consequently, this means the writs were simultaneously contracts securing the rank and status of the local officials and the strings by which the king could control them.

How Were the Divine Women Organized?

The preceding descriptions also applied to the divine women, or priestesses, in their roles as public religious figures with *noro* responsible for rituals in one or more subdistricts. The *noro* system was established in Amami and Okinawa, but in Sakishima, the women holding equivalent positions were called *tsukasa*. While there are no surviving documents to ascertain whether *tsukasa* received official appointments through writs, there were official priestesses, ranking higher than *noro*, known as *Miyako no ōamo* (great mother of Miyako) and *Yaeyama no ōamo* (great mother of Yaeyama).

As touched on in Chapter 2, in addition to the *ōamo* of Miyako and Yaeyama, there was the *kimihae* of Kumejima, *aoriyae* of Nakijin, *futakayata no amo* of Izena Island, and the *ōamo* of Naha, among others; we know the role also existed in Amami. Serving regions larger than single districts, some of these women had the privilege of regular audiences with the king. They all served in the king's name, as decreed by writs of appointment.

Ōamo and *noro* were both positions filled by local women to perform religious duties. The use of writs of appointment to install local divine women such as these signifies that, even though these were religious roles, the appointing authority belonged to the king, and through these appointments, the king was involved in managing the kingdom's religious rituals. In other words, by recognizing the official standing of those leading the rituals, the king structured them into an organizational framework.

At this point, I want to touch on the debate around the unity of politics and ritual in ancient Ryukyu, and to focus on this institution of divine women, which seems to have ranked equally with the executive government headed by the king. Researchers have advocated for this view since before the war, with some arguing strongly that ritual outweighed political matters. Some interpretations even try to bend this idea to fit the relationship between Queen Himiko of Yamatai-koku[4] and her younger brother. While it is valid to point out the importance of the divine women and the ritual observances within the structure of the Ryukyu Kingdom, any claims that they surpassed the king's authority seem to diverge from reality. To repeat, all the divine women, from the Kikoe Ōgimi (high priestess)[5] and down, held their position through royal writs issued under the authority of the king.

Guaranteed Sources of Income

With local officials on the executive side and local divine women on the ritual side, local governance of the kingdom was organized into a system through the writs of appointment. At the same time, however, these officials did not receive only a sheet of paper establishing their appointment; in writ A in the previous chapter, the newly appointed Gushikawa *noro*, Makatō, was also granted 50 *nuki* of farmland as a source of income.

---

4. Himiko, also known as Pimiko or Pimiku (ca. 170–248 CE), was a semi-legendary shamaness-queen in ancient Japan or Yamatai-koku, the precursor to what would come to be known as Yamato.
5. This position was held by the most senior divine woman, usually the mother, sister, or daughter of the king, who sat at the pinnacle of the religious structure.

THE ORGANIZATION OF THE KINGDOM

Every position and rank came with plots of land conferred by the king. From the extant writs of appointment, we can see that the combination of both the appointment and the accompanying economic benefits in a single document was more of an exception, and it is more likely that these were set out in separate documents and issued as a set.

This arrangement applied to central officials as well as local. The land granted to central officials such as the *ōyakomoi* class, and to prominent local officials (such as the Shuri *ōyako* and *ōyako*, and similar) was known as *satonushi dokoro* (master's domain). Farmland given to officials such as the *okite* with jurisdiction over subdistricts was called *okite no chi* (*okite*'s land). Finally, the fields and paddies granted to the *noro* and other divine women were called *noro kumoi chi* (lady priestess land), *noro chi* (priestess land), or *tonohara chi* (palace plain land), and so on. Whether male or female, anyone appointed to an official position by a writ of appointment, without exception, was also granted a guaranteed source of income by the king.

Fields and paddies were not the only form of grants. Depending on the rank of the position, the allocated farmland varied in area, often exceeding what the individual or their family could cultivate themselves. In these cases, the king allowed officials and divine women to have a specified number of dedicated laborers, and the right to requisition the labor of the local people, known as *temazukai* (lit. "hand labor").

The writs of appointment show that a variety of systems developed to support this compensation arrangement. As seen in writ A, the *noro kumoi chi* given to Makatō as a source of income had an area measured in units of *nuki*. In contrast, the area of rice paddies was measured in *kariya*, a different way of measuring the size of a field, which was worked through a system of required labor measured in units of *sukama*, meaning the work done in one day by one person. The kingdom had a unique system of measurements to provide compensation for divine women and local officials.

CHAPTER V

The *haruna* (lit. "field name") system, in which plots of land were named, served to clearly identify the locations of paddies and fields allocated to divine women and officials. Writ A indicates that Makatō was granted 50 *nuki* of farmland and goes on to note the names of the fields: Gushikawa-haru, Niyoha-baru, Hamakawa-haru, and Hoki-haru. The Ryukyuan world was divided into *magiri* (districts), and then further subdivided into *shima* (subdistricts); finally, the subdistricts were slivered into a system of named parcels of land, the *haruna*, with the smallest units closely related to the inhabitants' daily lives (this system is still used in present-day Okinawa). Because of this, we can assume that the Shuri royal government had a comprehensive and detailed land registry recording the *haruna* of all the cultivated land in its territory, and this record probably enabled the government to designate the fields to be granted to the divine women and officials.

The paddies and fields owned by common farmers, excluding the land granted to divine women and officials, were known as *mahito ji* (lit. "real person land"). All these lands, both *mahito ji* and the land held by divine women and officials, were assessed for the *mikanai*, a tax which had to be paid to the king. It's unclear how these taxes were assessed, what the rates were, and how collection was handled, but the writs of appointment show that in addition to paying in kind with grain and other harvest goods, region-specific products were also offered up in tribute.

In this way, the writs of appointment convey not only the existence of the divine women and officials serving the king and how they were compensated, but also provide a glimpse of how tax revenues were collected on behalf of the king.

THE ORGANIZATION OF THE KINGDOM

2. What Were *Hiki*?

Hiki *in the Writs of Appointment*

Shifting focus somewhat, let's peek into the reality of the Shuri royal government, the administrative organization of the Ryukyu Kingdom. First, look at the following writ of appointment:

E: Writ of Appointment Investing Fusaitomi *Hiki Gerae Akukabe* Shipmaster (1562)

> *Shiyori no [omikoto]*
> *[stamp] Fusaitomi ga hiki no*
>   *gerae akukabe no*
>   *sendō ha*
>   *Hae no kōri no*
>   *Hitori Ōmine no ōyakomoi ni*
> *[stamp] tamawari mōshi sōrō*
> *Shiyori yori Ōmine no ōyakomoi ga hō he mairu*
> *Kasei yonjū ichi nen jūni gatsu itsu ka*

> By order of Shuri
> As Fusaitomi *hiki* famous and splendid red-capped shipmaster, one *ōyakomoi* of Ōmine of the Southern Wind Armory Authority,
> Hereby ordered
> From Shuri to the honorable *ōyakomoi* of Ōmine delivered
> Jiajing 41st year, 12th month, 5th day

Based on the pattern of this writ, the above text is saying that the position of "*Fusaitomi ga hiki no gerae akukabe no sendō* (Fusaitomi *hiki*

145

CHAPTER V

famous and splendid red-capped shipmaster)" is being granted to the *"Hae no kōri no hitori Ōmine no ōyakomoi* (one *ōyakomoi* of Ōmine of the Southern Wind Armory Authority)." The term *gerae* in *gerae akukabe* is a beautifying prefix meaning "famous and splendid." *Akuka* refers to those with vermillion heads, that is, the group of low-ranking officials who wrapped their heads with vermillion headwear. As discussed in Chapter 2, the system of headwear color reflecting the rank of the wearer was established during the reign of King Shō Shin. *Sendō* (shipmaster) later came to be termed *sedō* (commander), meaning the leader of a specific organization. The *ōyakomoi* of Ōmine, Ōmine being a place name, as discussed earlier, was an official of the central government.

Here, the *ōyakomoi* of Ōmine, who had until then been part of the *Hae no kōri*, is being transferred to a position overseeing the officials of the *Fusaitomi ga hiki*, making *Fusaitomi ga hiki* and *Hae no kōri* seem like the key words here. We'll start by first examining the mysterious term *Fusaitomi ga hiki*.

Fusaitomi ga hiki can be broken into three main parts, *fusai*, *tomi*, and *hiki*— the *ga* here being equivalent to the possessive *no* in modern Japanese. *Fusai* is a Ryukyuan beautifying prefix meaning "fitting" or "suitable," and *tomi*, a contracted form of *toyomi*, is a beautifying term suggesting fame and splendor. So, what is the meaning of the word *hiki*?

Written Sources on Shuri Castle's Royal Guard

The word *hiki*, distributed throughout the regions of Amami, Okinawa, and Sakishima, relates to the organizational principles of family or ritual groups, and is of interest to the fields of anthropology and folklore studies. Possibly its meaning refers to something of shared interest, but the issue here is *hiki* as an organizing element within the royal government.

THE ORGANIZATION OF THE KINGDOM

According to the *Ryūkyū-koku yuraiki* (compiled in 1713), which records the origins and history of Ryukyu, *hiki* refers to the royal guard garrison of Shuri Castle. Next the text says that the origin of the *hiki* system is unclear, but that in ancient Ryukyu there were twelve units of royal guards (*hiki*) with a commander called the *sedō*, and a second-in-command called the *chikudūn*, both once of relatively high rank. However, during the structural reforms in the late seventeenth century, three units were eliminated, reducing the total to nine, and both the *sedō* and *chikudūn* ranks were downgraded.

Table 3 on page 148 charts the information about the remaining nine royal guard units as recorded in the *Ryūkyū-koku yuraiki*. These remaining nine units are listed in the column titled "*Hiki* name," all with honorific titles. Among them is the Fusaitomi *hiki* that appeared earlier in Writ E. The column "Personnel" lists the names and number of positions within each unit.

In a traditional system that had continued from the time of ancient Ryukyu, the garrison was divided into three shifts based on the names of the days they were on duty: guard of the ox, snake, and rooster. Each shift worked on their assigned days. The chart groups the nine units by their respective days on duty. Among these, the lead *hiki*, the *hikigashira*, in the guard of the ox was Seiyaritomi; in the guard of the snake, Jakunitomi; and in the guard of the rooster, Sejiaratomi. The "Notes" section of the table lists the three *hiki* eliminated in the late seventeenth century, Kumokotomi, Yotsugitomi, and Amaetomi. Unfortunately, except for Yotsugitomi, we don't know which guard shift these belonged to. However, in ancient Ryukyu, before the reformation that eliminated them, each of the three likely belonged to one of the three guard shifts, bringing each one up to four *hiki* in total.

Each *hiki* had personnel of various positions ranked below the commander and second-in-command. These personnel held relatively

CHAPTER V

Table 3. *Hiki* Names and Personnel

	Hiki name	Personnel
Guard of the Ox	Seiyaritomi (lead *hiki*)	*azana* (2), *nakajō sedō* (1), *nakajō* (1), *gerai akukabe* (11), *jōjūsha* (1)
	Sedakatomi	*azana* (3), *nakajō* (1), *gerai akukabe* (10), *jōjūsha* (1)
	Ukitoyomi	*azana* (3), *nakajō* (1), *gerai akukabe* (10), *toki* (3), *jōjūsha* (1)
Guard of the Snake	Jakunitomi (lead *hiki*)	*azana* (3), *nakajō sedō* (1), *nakajō* (1), *gerai akukabe* (10)
	Shimauchitomi	*azana* (3), *nakajō* (1), *gerai akukabe* (10)
	Oshiaketomi	*azana* (3), *nakajō* (1), *gerai akukabe* (9), *jōjūsha* (3), *toki* (1)
Guard of the Rooster	Sejiaratomi (lead *hiki*)	*azana* (4), *nakajō sedō* (1), *nakajō* (2), *gerai akukabe* (14)
	Fusaitomi	*azana* (4), *nakajō* (2), *gerai akukabe* (12), *jōjūsha* (3), *saji* (2)
	Yomochitomi	*azana* (10), *nakajō* (8), *gokyōbu* (38)
Notes	Eliminated *hiki*: Kumokotomi, Yotsugitomi, Amaetomi	

Based on *Ryūkyū-koku yuraiki*, Vol. 2.

low ranks, and their main duty was to guard Shuri Castle. For example, *azana* referred to the sentries stationed on the observation platforms on the castle's eastern and western outer walls. *Nakajō sedō* oversaw command of the *nakajō*, guards stationed at the central gate. *Gerai akukabe* were guards identified by their red headwear while *jōjūsha* were guards permanently stationed at Shuri Castle. Officials known as *toki* scheduled and managed important events and technicians called *saji* were responsible for castle maintenance and repair. *Gokyōbu* attended to the transportation needs of those leaving the castle by bearing them in palanquins.

A Difference in Meaning: Writs of Appointment vs. Ryūkyū-koku yuraiki

If we interpret the section in writ E concerning the *hiki* based on the previous analysis of what is in the *Ryūkyū-koku yuraiki*, then it means "appointed famous and splendid vermillion-capped commander of the Fusaitomi royal guard unit." However, no matter how many times I repeat this interpretation, I remain unconvinced. My concern is that this source of information was far removed from the circumstances around the writ. There is a broad discrepancy between the image drawn by the writs of appointment of ancient Ryukyu, and the depiction of the *hiki* as recorded in the *Ryūkyū-koku yuraiki*.

The writs of appointment of ancient Ryukyu show that officials from Amami Ōshima belonged to the Jakunitomi. Furthermore, they held positions as *okite* in subdistrict (called *sawa* instead of *shima* in Amami Ōshima) administrations and could rise to the position of *ōyako*. In another writ, a person affiliated with the Seiyaritomi was appointed to serve as staff on tribute ships making the crossing to China, actually traveling overseas for work. In other words, this differs greatly from the image in the *Ryūkyū-koku yuraiki* portraying the *hiki* as the royal guard of Shuri Castle. In addition, because writ E shows a central government official of the *ōyakomoi* class being appointed as shipmaster of a *hiki*, the *hiki* of ancient Ryukyu must have differed from those of later times. Just why the head of the *hiki* was called a shipmaster is a perplexing question.

Here, let us turn our attention to the report in the *Ryūkyū-koku yuraiki* of the late-seventeenth century reforms that reduced the number of *hiki* and downgraded the rank of their commanders and seconds-in-command. The implication is that the *hiki* as portrayed in the *Ryūkyū-koku yuraiki* represents their function in the early eighteenth century, after the earlier reforms that reduced their numbers and their leaders' status; and that we must develop a very different image of the *hiki* of ancient Ryukyu that existed before the changes.

Why the Connection with Trade Ships?

Amid the overwhelming scarcity of historical documents, the biggest clues regarding the *hiki* can be found in the writs of appointment from ancient Ryukyu. Consider the following:

F: Writ of Appointment Investing *Yotsugitomi* Shipmaster of China Trading Ship (1537)

> *Shiyori no omi [koto]*
> *[stamp] Tau he mai [ru]*
>   *Yotsugitomi ga sen [dō ha]*
>   *Hae no kōri [no]*
>   *Hitori Ameku no ōya [kumoi ni]*
> *[stamp] tamawari mōshi [sōrō]*
> *Shiyori yori Ameku no ōyakumoi ga [hō he mairu]*
> *Kasei jūroku nen hachi gatsu [hatsu ka]*

> By order of Shuri
> For travel to Tang, as shipmaster of *Yotsugitomi*, one *ōyakomoi* of Ameku of the Southern Wind Armory Authority,
> Hereby ordered

> From Shuri to the honorable *ōyakomoi* of Ameku delivered Jiajing 16th year, 8th month, 20th day

To translate, this writ appoints the *ōyakomoi* of Ameku of the Southern Wind Armory Authority as shipmaster of a vessel named *Yotsugitomi* to be dispatched to Tang (China). Because the person sailing by trade ship to China was appointed to this task via a writ of appointment from the king, this document proves without question that Ryukyu's overseas trade was a national enterprise carried out under the king's patronage.

Setting that aside, let's take a careful look at the wording. The vessel making the voyage to China was called *Yotsugitomi*, the same name as one of the three eliminated *hiki* in the "Notes" section of Table 3. In addition, on this trading ship *Yotsugitomi*, there is a position of shipmaster that has been awarded to the *ōyakomoi* of Ameku, an official of the central government. Why do the *hiki* and the trading ship have the same name? Again, why does the leader of the *hiki* share the title of *sendō* with the shipmaster? In another example of this, a different writ of appointment grants the position of *chikudono* (second-in-command)[6] to a person named Masaburo Tekogu on the *Sejiaratomi*, a trading ship dispatched to Southeast Asia. *Sejiaratomi* matches the name of one of the *hiki* listed as part of the guard of the rooster in Table 3. In other words, not only did the ships' names match, but the titles of positions aboard the ships were also identical to those of *hiki* personnel.

Why did the forms fall together like this? To explore the matter, I turned to the *Omoro sōshi*, an anthology of ancient Ryukyuan ritual songs. As an example, an *omoro* in volume three of the *Omoro sōshi* contains the following verses as a prayer for safe navigation:

---

6. The title of *chikudono* was an archaic form of *chikudūn*, the second-in-command of a *hiki*, having changed much like the title of *sendō* (shipmaster) later became *sedō*.

Mata	*Yohikitomi oshi ukete*
	Sejiaratomi oshi ukete
Mata	*Yotsugitomi oshi ukete*
	Kumokotomi oshi ukete
Mata	*Amaetomi oshi ukete*
	Oshiaketomi oshi ukete

The term *oshi ukete* means the launch of a ship out to sea. The six names from *Yohikitomi* to *Oshiaketomi* are all ships' names, and except for the first one, *Yohikitomi*, they all correspond to the names of *hiki* listed in Table 3. A song from volume thirteen of the *Omoro sōshi* has a short preface recording that on the twenty-fifth day of the eleventh month of 1517, when a trading ship named *Sejiaratomi* set sail for Southeast Asia, King Shō Shin himself sang the *omoro* blessing. This confirms, once again, that *Sejiaratomi* was undoubtedly the name of a ship.

Trade Ships on Land

The large ships of Ryukyu intended for the overseas trade were given at least three types of names. The first type of name reflected the license used to verify ships' registration under the public trading system, with examples like *Kyōjigō-sen* and *Eijigō-kaisen*. The second type were perfectly ordinary, such as *Koshira Maru* or *Takara Maru*. The third type, and our focus here, were eulogistic names using poetic beautifying terms from the Ryukyuan language, such as *Yotsugitomi, Sejiaratomi*, and so on. The first two types of names appear in diplomatic documents recorded in the *Rekidai hōan* and were recognized in the international community. However, the third type are found only in sources such as the writs of appointment and the *Omoro sōshi* that are specific to Ryukyu.

THE ORGANIZATION OF THE KINGDOM

In Ryukyu, there were fascinating customs related to ships. For example, shipbuilding was apparently likened to a bird sitting on her eggs to keep them warm until the hatchlings emerged, raising them until they were old enough to leave the nest. From this, shipbuilding sites were also called *sura jo*, meaning "nest-hatching place." *Sura* is thought to originate from the term *suderu*, or "to hatch." The moment a ship was launched from the *sura jo* was called the *sura oroshi* (nest-hatch drop), and ships at sea were compared to birds of prey such as eagles and falcons. All Ryukyuan trading ships had large eyes painted on either side of the bow, likely meant to represent the piercing gaze of these birds. Many religious songs call for the ships to be as ferocious and majestic as eagles and falcons as they navigate across the vast ocean.

Divine women leading the launching ceremonies probably gave the ships their poetic names, which are thought to have deep connections with the world of Ryukyuan ritual ceremony and prayer. The ritual songs about ships and maritime voyages in the *Omoro sōshi* provide insight into this.

With this understanding, we can't deny that *Yotsugitomi*, *Sejiaratomi*, and others, must have been ship names before they were the names of royal guard units, just as *sendō* and *chikudono* were crew positions on a ship before they were titles. This raises the question: why were the names of seafaring ships transferred to the *hiki*, which were most likely to have been land-based organizations?

I propose the following explanation: The land-based royal guard modeled their organization after the system of maritime navigation and crew structure found on trading vessels, in effect creating a land-based version of a trading ship. Only through this understanding can we explain the curious similarities between the names and ranks of the *hiki* and the ships' crews.

This hypothesis is supported by the examination of the Ryukyu Kingdom's military organization in the next section.

CHAPTER V

3. The Military Defense Structure and the *Kōri-Hiki* System

The Military Defense Structure as Depicted in Inscriptions

Shuri Castle and Naha Port were the pivotal centers of the kingdom, and there must have been some form of defense system established for both locations. Unfortunately, records from that period are extremely rare, with only a few limited inscriptions available.

According to the inscription on the Madama Port monument, erected in 1522 during the reign of King Shō Shin, a road was constructed that year to connect Shuri Castle and Toyomi Gusuku, with the Madan Bridge spanning the Kokuba River. The purpose of this civil engineering project was to allow the rapid deployment of troops to Toyomi Gusuku, a key point in the defense of Naha Port, and to ensure that defensive forces could be quickly sent to what was then known as the Netatehi River (a freshwater spring later known as the Utinda), a vital source of water for sailors and residents in Naha.

The next inscription, from a monument built at Yarazamori Gusuku during the reign of King Shō Sei in 1554, states that in the event of an attack by a foreign enemy, three groups were to mobilize: the Shuri Castle Defense Unit, the Naha City Defense Unit, and the defense forces on the south bank of Naha Port at Kakinohana (located on the Netatehi River) and Yarazamori Gusuku. This army, composed of three separate units, presumably royal guard units, was to be augmented along the line of defense by military personnel from Shimajiri, the southern part of Okinawa Island, during military operations.

From the scant description provided by these inscriptions, we can infer the existence of a regular standing army organized in the central strategic areas of Shuri and Naha, a force composed of the previously mentioned three rotating guard shifts of ox, snake, and rooster, and that a reserve force in the Shimajiri region could be mobilized in times of emergency. The standing army was likely composed of the royal guard, and given the nature of military operations, we can assume the reserve force also had some kind of association with the *hiki*. This assumption is based on the fact that, like the *okite* official in the Sawa subdistrict of Amami who was affiliated with the Jakunitomi *hiki*, it is reasonable to assume that local residents, including local officials, were mobilized into the royal government's military system through their *hiki* organizations.

As the kingdom's trading ships plied back and forth between various Asian countries, they often faced the threat of attack from pirates during their voyages. Naturally, the organization of the crew sailing on these ships included personnel needed to protect the vessels in times of such emergencies. The *hiki*, believe to be modeled after the crew organization of maritime vessels, likely also took on their military character in confronting and repelling invaders who attacked via land.

Presumably, the *hiki* organizations of ancient Ryukyu had the responsibility of ensuring the safety of ships while at sea and oversaw the security and smooth operation of political and administrative matters on land. The *hiki* of the early modern period depicted in the *Ryūkyūkoku yuraiki* retained their defensive and security characteristics, but the overall role of the system seems to have diminished by that time.

What Were the Kōri?

The *hiki* of ancient Ryukyu, however, cannot be reduced to just a military organization. They must have had a general political and administrative side as well, as can be understood from writ E when it mentions "*Hae no kōri.*" *Hae* means "southern wind," and *kōri*,[7] with possible meanings of "armory authority" or "storehouse authority," gives us "southern wind armory authority" or similar. And from its mentions in the writs of appointment, *Hae no kōri* seems to have been an administrative body within Shuri Castle.

In addition to the *Hae no kōri*, the writs of appointment also mention *Nishi no kōri* (northern armory authority).[8] There is a single instance of a third *kōri* that is neither of these. However, and very regrettably, several characters making up a crucial part of the name are completely illegible. If we allow this unidentified *kōri* to be called "X *kōri*," then the writs only mention these three *kōri*: The Southern Wind *kōri*, the Northern *kōri*, and the X *kōri*. We can presume that these would have been high-level administrative entities within Shuri Castle.

The Kōri-Hiki *System*

Notably, most of the officials belonging to the *kōri* were central officials of the *ōyakomoi* class. In addition, there are many instances of these officials being appointed as commanders of the royal guard with the title of *sendō* or *sedō*.

For example, the *ōyakomoi* of Ōmine who received writ E belonged to the Southern Wind *kōri*, and it granted him the position of commander for the Fusaitomi *hiki*. Additionally, in a second extant writ of appointment granted a year later, in 1563, this same *ōyakomoi* of Ōmine is still a member of the Southern Wind *kōri*, but another writ names him as the commander of the Sejiaratomi *hiki*. This writ is an

---

7. This term would later be written with the Chinese characters 庫理, which can be read as *kuri*.
8. Here, *nishi* is the archaic Okinawan reading for 北 (north).

example of a personnel transfer from one *hiki* to another. It provides an important clue for understanding the relationship between *kōri* and *hiki*. The fact that personnel could be transferred to a different *hiki* while remaining in the same *kōri* suggests that a *kōri* had multiple *hiki* under its jurisdiction. In other words, *kōri* were higher-level organizations with the *hiki* as subordinate groups.

With this in mind, a fresh look at the writs of appointment makes it clear that at one time, the three *kōri* oversaw the twelve *hiki* during the ancient Ryukyu period. Furthermore, each of the three were senior over a group of four *hiki*. We saw in Table 3 how the *hiki* were divided into three groups, and the three guard shifts corresponded to the three *kōri*. This tripartite grouping gives us a vague understanding that each of the *kōri* were under the supervision of a member of the Yo'asutabe (Council of Three).

An organizational chart showing the above is laid out on page 158. I've named this chart the *kōri-hiki* system. It's a small detail that I have managed to make out about the obscure and distant Shuri royal government of ancient Ryukyu. The paramount authority overseeing this system was, of course, the king.

Becoming a central official associated with a *kōri* or being granted the rank of commander or second-in-command of a *hiki* through a writ of appointment, indicates that, in the light of the general principle of such documents, *kōri* and *hiki* were distinct organizational entities that assumed a system of appointments and personnel transfers. In particular, the *hiki*, as a kind of land-based trading ship's crew organized in a militaristic fashion, seems to have been a unique organization suited to the Ryukyu Kingdom as a trading nation extending its influence across the seas.

It is, however, important to clarify here that the *kōri-hiki* system depicted in the organizational chart is not meant to represent the entirety of the central government institutions of the Ryukyu Kingdom.

CHAPTER V

Figure 7. **The *Kōri-Hiki* System**

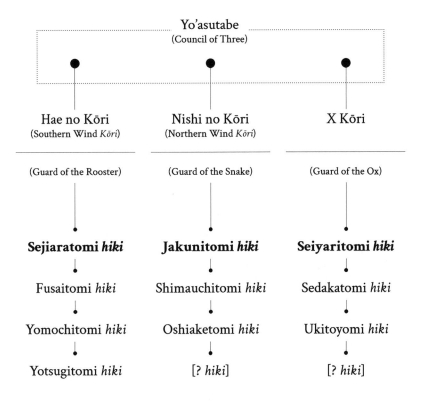

Note: The spaces marked [?] were probably Kumokotomi *hiki* and Amaetomi *hiki* but at the time of this writing neither could be ascertained. Bold characters indicate the *hikigashira*, or lead *hiki*.

If we had all of the writs of appointment, the actual Shuri government would very likely have had a more complex organization, with a much greater variety of named sections and positions. Just to stress the point, we must keep in mind that the fifty-eight writs of appointment remaining from the period of ancient Ryukyu provide us with only a rough image of its administrative structure.

The Writs as a Symbol of Ryukyu's Identity

Now, having conducted this examination of the writs of appointment of ancient Ryukyu, there is one last issue to address: their symbolic nature.

Why were they written in the hiragana script? Other records from ancient Ryukyu written with hiragana notation include the *Omoro sōshi*, inscriptions on monuments, and epitaphs engraved on the stone coffins of the elite class. However, the fact that the writs of appointment, official documents issued in enormous numbers, were also written in hiragana is of great significance. Probably the main reason is that hiragana is a phonetic script, making it a useful tool to convey information, in a way that Chinese characters, as an ideographic script, may not have been. This is instantly obvious in considering how the divine songs collected in the *Omoro sōshi*, no matter what effort was made, could not be written in classical Chinese.

But that is not the only reason. It's instantly evident that the wording of the writs of appointment quoted here, even if it includes some phrasings peculiar to the Ryukyuan language, is fundamentally not that different from the classical and formal style of Japanese in the late medieval period. Looked at in a certain way, it can be understood as a medieval Japanese text in a regional dialect. As a result, in addition to seeing hiragana as a convenient tool due to its phonetic script, we

CHAPTER V

must also recognize a sense of "same text, same people" in the writs, implying a deep affinity with Japan.

According to linguistics research, it appears that the formation of the "central language," the political language of Shuri, began around the time Shō Hashi unified Sanzan and established the Ryukyu Kingdom. In the diverse linguistic landscape of Ryukyu, where each island or region spoke its own local dialect, the adoption of a common language beyond the dialects useful only in narrow communities became essential in order to convey the king's orders throughout the territory, and to send messages and reports of all kinds back to Shuri. In short, it was the dialect spoken in Shuri, formed in response to political and administrative needs, that became the Ryukyu Kingdom's common language. That the Shuri dialect as expressed in the writs of appointment was essentially a variation of medieval Japanese is an important fact.

Another point is that the writs, without exception, give their dates of issuance in terms of the Chinese imperial era. After King Satto sent his first tribute delegation in 1372, Ryukyu as a Chinese tributary vassal began to use the Chinese calendar, essentially a requirement for tribute states. The principle of using the Chinese era name is consistent across all records, not only in the diplomatic records in the *Rekidai hōan*, but also in inscriptions on monuments and stone coffins, and in the *Omoro sōshi* and writs of appointment. By stating the date of issuance in this way, the writs of appointment symbolically represented the real relationship between Ryukyu and China.

The writs of appointment describe a world with a fundamentally Japanese cultural consciousness leavened with an awareness of China in actual diplomatic relations. From this understanding, the last point I wish to make here rests on a question. In whose name, exactly, were these documents created, and for what purpose? Obviously, they were not created in the name of Japan, nor were they issued for the sake of China. They were official, public documents issued by the king of

THE ORGANIZATION OF THE KINGDOM

Ryukyu to administer the Ryukyu Kingdom. The core subject of the writs began and ended with the king, and these documents were used to govern the kingdom. In this regard, the cultural consciousness shared with Japan, and the diplomatic relations focused on China, as expressed in the writs of appointment, are ultimately just ancillary issues.

In this understanding, the Ryukyu Kingdom asserts its organizational structure in the writs of appointment, and at the same time, the writs themselves give a clear display of the Ryukyu Kingdom's sense of its own identity.

Conclusion

1. What Ancient Ryukyu Represents

"A foreign nation within the Japanese bakuhan *system"*

I believe the following points have been largely clarified by the description developed above.

The society of the Ryukyu Islands originated from a common cultural foundation shared with the people in the Japanese archipelago. This island society gradually underwent a process of individualization and by the time of the ancient Ryukyu period, an independent kingdom clearly distinct from the Japanese nation had emerged. This kingdom shaped its own history as it engaged with Asia's international community. Furthermore, the kingdom had its own distinct systems and organizations for governing domestic affairs.

This kingdom that had emerged to the south of mainland Japan eventually became integrated into the Japanese nation in incremental steps. The first step in the process occurred in the early modern period with the Shimazu Invasion of 1609. Broadly speaking, the Ryukyu Kingdom became part of the early modern Japanese polity (the feudal *bakuhan* system), with the Satsuma domain holding direct administrative power over it. For example, Satsuma introduced fundamental policies of the *bakuhan* system that had a powerful effect on reshaping the kingdom's structure: the prohibition on Christianity, the policy of national isolation, the system to determine land value for taxation purposes, and the social policy that organized and divided the population into the samurai, peasant, artisan, and merchant classes. In effect, the

CONCLUSION

kingdom took on new characteristics throughout the early modern period to become "Ryukyu within the *bakuhan* system."

However, the royal government system of Ryukyu also remained intact. The kingdom continued to receive Chinese imperial envoys—the Qing emperor sending envoys after the fall of the Ming—and continued to send tribute missions to China. Thus, the kingdom retained its age-old characteristics of "Ryukyu as kingdom" and "Ryukyu as tributary nation." These two traits survived as vibrant elements of the kingdom's identity as it progressed through the early modern period under the *bakuhan* system.

In reality, the kingdom was a subordinate entity incorporated into the national polity of early modern Japan while simultaneously appearing to act as a vassal in the Chinese system of imperial investiture—a rather ambiguous existence for the kingdom in the early modern period at first glance. Many historians have described this situation as *Nis-Shi ryōzoku*, or the "Japan-China dual affiliation." Although this description is not entirely wrong, the manner of affiliation with Japan was a direct one centered around a relationship of domination and subordination. The affiliation with China occurred indirectly through diplomacy and trade, so the term "dual affiliation," implying similar levels of influence, cannot be considered accurate. In addition, even though Ryukyu was subordinate to the Japanese feudal system and continued to receive investiture from the Chinese emperor, direct governance of the land and people was carried out by the king and his governing institution, the Shuri royal government. Accordingly, to take into account this multi-faceted situation, recent historians have come to express the fundamental nature of early modern Ryukyu as "a foreign nation within the Japanese *bakuhan* system."

The second step of integration came as a result of Ryukyu's annexation, when the kingdom was abolished and Okinawa Prefecture

CONCLUSION

was established in 1879. Eight years earlier, in 1871, Japan had abolished the *han* system and established its prefectures on the premise of the 1869 decision to return the lands and people controlled by each daimyo to the emperor.[1] However, in the case of Ryukyu, the king had never received the right to rule over the land and people from the Japanese emperor in the first place, so there was no need to "return" the land and people. Faced with strong opposition from Ryukyu against the establishment of Okinawa Prefecture and vigorous protests based on its suzerainty over Ryukyu from China, the Meiji government consequently had no choice but to mobilize military and police forces from the mainland and seize and occupy Shuri Castle by force. Had the kingdom been fully incorporated into Japan during the 270-year long early modern period, perhaps this contentious situation would not have occurred. The conflict between the three parties—Ryukyu, Japan, and China—over the establishment of Okinawa Prefecture can be attributed to the fact that the kingdom continued its nominal existence as a foreign nation during the early modern period, even as it was, in reality, under the control of the Japanese feudal system.

Why Is Okinawa a Part of Japan?

In this way, the region became a part of Japanese society as half the land under the kingdom's rule was forcibly incorporated into the Japanese polity upon the Shimazu Invasion at the beginning of the early modern period. The other half followed suit with the annexation of Ryukyu at the beginning of the modern era. The underlying framework that

---

1. The Meiji Restoration in 1868 was followed by the Boshin War, a civil war between forces loyal to the Tokugawa shogunate and a coalition force representing the Imperial Court.

determined this incorporation into Japanese society came out of the Ryukyu Kingdom that had developed earlier during the ancient Ryukyu era.

However, the historical significance of ancient Ryukyu has been consistently undervalued, and since before World War II, the historical narrative has dismissed or camouflaged its importance. For example, based on the legend that Shunten (r. 1187–1237), the "first king of Ryukyu," was the son of Minamoto no Tametomo, many historians have argued that the kings of Ryukyu belonged to the lineage of the Seiwa Genji, and thus what at first glance appears to have been a unique historical process really just falls under the umbrella of Japanese history. Other researchers have asserted that Ryukyu appeared distinctive only because it was at the periphery, geographically distant from the center, and that Ryukyu's unique story essentially fell within the larger framework of Japanese regional history. Further, there are experts who claim that Japan and Okinawa have shared the same language and identity since ancient times, resulting in a strong sense of affinity that prevents the two from regarding each other as foreign nations.

This historical narrative persisted even during the postwar occupation period, and amid the swirling movement in Okinawa for the return to Japan (or, from the perspective of mainland Japan, for the reversion of Okinawa). It can be said that rather than being disputed, this narrative became accepted in an ambiguous way. At this time, Japan had been divided in two: the mainland under the postwar constitution of Japan, and Okinawa under US administration. The most urgent political focus was on reunification, to end this division as soon as possible, and return Okinawa to the homeland under the postwar constitution. Consequently, questions about how this "homeland" was formed, and how its history was related to Okinawa, were pushed aside.

The instant response to the question, "Why should Okinawa return to Japan?" was "Because it is Japanese." A second question, "So, how is it Japanese?" kicked off a search for evidence supporting why Okinawa was a part of Japan. Examples of this evidence included stories like the origin legend about Minamoto Tametomo, the ideology of Okinawa as just a region of Japan, or ideas about shared language and identity, and so on. With this imprecise historical narrative still in place, on May 15, 1972, nonetheless, Okinawa reverted to Japan.

During the five years after reversion, up until 1977, various opinion polls found that only about half of all Okinawans answered that they were glad to return. Now, however, the majority of residents in Okinawa share this sentiment. If most Okinawans desired the return to Japan, and most of them eventually said they were satisfied with that result, it is the responsibility of historians to reconstruct the historical narrative against the backdrop of public opinion. On the basis that Okinawa is now a part of Japan, historians have the duty of taking up the fundamental issue of exploring why Okinawa is Japanese, and if so, what kind of "Japan" narrative we should aim for.

The Need for a New Narrative in Japanese History

In my book *Ryūkyū no jidai* (The Age of Ryukyu), I wrote that "the study of ancient Ryukyu is a study of 'foreign history' for [the field of] Japanese history." Even now, my position on this has not changed. Upon reading this observation, several researchers have half-jokingly asked whether I was a proponent of "Ryukyuan independence."

I am indeed a proponent of the idea of Ryukyuan independence. I stress the fact that although the Okinawan people share linguistic and ethnic ancestry with those in Japan, Okinawa, as ancient Ryukyu, established an independent kingdom that was clearly distinct from the medieval state in the Japanese archipelago. I reject the flat historical narrative that places this land under the umbrella of Japanese history

CONCLUSION

by claiming that it was ruled by a descendant of Minamoto Tametomo; that this was a part of Japan that developed its unique history because of its location in the periphery; that an "affinity" with the Japanese archipelago prevented people here from regarding Japan as a foreign nation. I hold that these and similar arguments are nothing more than a kind of ideology that ignores the reality of the course of history.

Unfortunately, the conventional narratives that Japan has evolved under a single-nation framework since the dawn of history and that the Japanese people have been a single homogenous ethnic group since time immemorial have persisted up until now. Prevailing ethnic theories and the like mean that the traditional view of Japanese history has had a strong tendency to dismiss diversity. When the significance of ancient Ryukyu cannot be appreciated, my only option is to maintain that "the study of ancient Ryukyu is a study of 'foreign history' for the field of Japanese history."

Ifa Fuyū once aptly pointed out in *Ko Ryūkyū no seiji* (The Politics of Ancient Ryukyu) that the study of Ryukyuan history lies in examining "how this branch of the Japanese ethnic group changed in response to its different circumstances," and in making clear the process by which this group has rejoined the entity called Japan, having become "the distinctive Ryukyuan people" during the ancient Ryukyu period. To borrow Ifa's expression, it is crucial to recognize how they became "the distinctive Ryukyuan people," and not only to talk about how they were "a branch of the Japanese ethnic group" to be incorporated back into Japan. In my opinion, the ideas expressed by Ifa Fuyū and Kawakami Hajime, discussed in Chapter 1, call for a stance in which diversity as an attribute of Japanese society must be recognized.

Given the highly individual history of Ryukyu, including the ancient Ryukyu era, I believe there is a need for a new narrative in Japanese history. Ryukyu's history should not be crammed into the conventional narrative of Japanese history, but rather, incorporated in a way that enriches the overall historical view of Japan. The history of Ryukyu should raise bold questions about the shape a new narrative would take. The Okinawan perspective must be included in order to allow for the fundamental understanding that Japanese society has not been a monolithic entity since ancient times, but has been continually reshaped as it absorbed various diverse influences, and even now is still evolving as a society. Looking back at history, it is important to honestly acknowledge the fact that during the era of ancient Ryukyu (the medieval period), the existence of an independent Ryukyu Kingdom means that during this time, Japan was composed of at least two different entities with distinct national forms. A vitally important point from the perspective of Ryukyuan history is that in the process of incorporating the Ryukyu Kingdom, the nature of Japan's polity and its society were both, in turn, also reshaped. We must emphasize that this region, distinctive due to its history as a kingdom, broadened the content of Japanese society as well as the framework of Japan's historical narrative as it became a part of Japan. In other words, the addition of Ryukyu/Okinawa's unique qualities gave form to Japan's society.

2. For the Sake of Restoration

The Historian as Producer

I made a conscious decision to become actively engaged outside the confines of my office, to go beyond just my research on the Ryukyu Kingdom. When invited to speak, I attended many different kinds of gatherings as time permitted to explain the importance of a new take on Ryukyuan history or of finding a new narrative of the kingdom. I contributed extensively to local newspapers and appeared on television and radio as often as possible to talk about the need to reevaluate Ryukyuan history from a new perspective. I even hosted a talk show on local FM radio dedicated to Ryukyu's history. My intention was to avoid confining my message about a new historical narrative to just a handful of like-minded colleagues, and to fulfill my duty as an Okinawan historian by getting it out to a wider public audience. My goal was to offer topics that could put the historical narrative of victimization into a greater context, so that Okinawans would not continue to be constrained by or subject only to dark and tortured history. For the same reason, a group of fellow enthusiasts and I planned a rock music festival.

After the war, there were rock musicians among those who earned their livelihoods by entertaining American soldiers. Many of them born to US soldiers and Okinawan mothers (known colloquially as *hāfu*, i.e., biracial), they performed brilliant American- and British-influenced rock music in clubs and live houses in the entertainment districts and on the military bases. To be sure, their music belonged to the genre of hard rock; nevertheless, it was rooted in the cultural environment of Okinawa, and so naturally conveyed a characteristic Okinawan flavor. Supergroups born out of the Okinawan postwar rock scene include bands like Murasaki and Condition Green, both known nationwide in the 1970s, and Medusa, led by Marie Kyan in the 1980s. Talking with these musicians and listening to their live performances led me to believe that their music was an unmistakable product of the occupation era, a creative achievement born out of that time. The era of US rule is usually portrayed almost exclusively in a negative way, focusing on land seizures for base construction, numerous crimes committed by military personnel, the suppression of human rights, and more. While these events are undeniable facts, I can't help but wonder if, instead of groaning about our victimhood, we instead grasped at something creative and positive in the midst of such harsh times. I came to this new perspective through Okinawan rock music.

CONCLUSION

It was also necessary to take a more positive approach in reevaluating postwar history. To that end, I persuaded administrators of the "base towns," and with the collaboration of government officials, musicians, and volunteers, we organized the Peaceful Love Rock Festival. Starting in 1984, this festival features performances by over twenty bands over two days and has become a major concert event adorning the hot Okinawan summer. The festival is a confirmation of the existence of a culture born during the postwar occupation era right here where we stand.

To reexamine our own history, we must actively embrace it as our own achievement; and to spread the idea of this new approach, historians have no choice but to become powerful activists. We need to play the role of producers in the movement to reassess history.

Immersed in the Restoration of Shuri Castle

Since the 1985 decision to use national funding to restore Shuri Castle, destroyed by fire in the Battle of Okinawa, I have been responsible for conducting historical research in support of the restoration project. In addition, I have worked hard in analyzing documents to provide our young architects with the information needed for the restoration. Shuri Castle itself was completely lost in the war, and when we started, it seemed that all related documents had been scattered and lost. At the beginning of the project, we had no idea how much of the castle could be restored, and to be honest, we felt considerable anxiety. However, our top priority was thorough and systematic data collection, and then to meticulously extract every bit of information we could from the documents we found.

In a pinch, a solution sometimes presents itself, and in this case, unexpectedly, we came upon a wealth of materials. For example, when the

CONCLUSION

seiden, the main hall of Shuri Castle, was dismantled for repairs, blueprints dating from the early Shōwa era (1926–89) were found in the archives of the Agency for Cultural Affairs. In addition, while I knew that major repairs had been carried out on the *seiden* in the mid-eighteenth century, I actually found ancient documents from that time, including construction reports, in the Kamakura Collection at the Okinawa Prefectural University of Arts. Finding these valuable documents allowed us to feel fairly confident in our ability to restore the *seiden*. However, for other structures such as the north hall (*hokuden*), the south hall (*nanden*), the guardhouse, and the Hōshin Gate, no such documents were to be found. As a consequence, we had no choice but to use concrete to build the basic structures, and then restore only the outer facades to their old appearances based on prewar photographs.

The restoration work proceeded smoothly thanks to the efforts of the many people involved, and the central part of the reconstructed Shuri Castle has been open to the public as Shurijō Kōen (Shuri Castle Park) since November 1992. Through the seven years of restoration, I immersed myself in the daily tasks related to the work. Certainly, I felt strongly that it was my responsibility as a living person to help recover the cultural heritage lost in the war. I was also personally motivated by my desire to exhaustively study Shuri Castle during this process. However, more than anything else, I was absolutely convinced that even if I were to write thousands of books, or to give tens of thousands of lectures about the significance of Ryukyuan history, my words would never have the impact of a restored Shuri Castle. With our tangible cultural heritage reduced to ashes in the Battle of Okinawa, there were no visible, physical structures left to attest to our unique history in the eyes of onlookers. If we could revive Shuri Castle, surely it would serve as a convincing backdrop to help others share in the ideas advocated by a simple historian. It was with such thoughts that I devoted myself to the restoration of Shuri Castle.

CONCLUSION

Shuri Castle was the heart of the Ryukyu Kingdom. It was the royal palace where the king and his family lived, functioning as the locus for politics, administration, diplomacy, and trade. It was the stage upon which were born the performing arts that were the core of the Ryukyuan kingdom's culture and was the most important center for the solemn religious rituals conducted by the Kikoe Ōgimi, the kingdom's highest-ranking priestess. In every sense, Shuri Castle stood as a symbol of the kingdom. Its restoration should make it easy to convey the fact that a unique kingdom once existed in the land of Okinawa.

Seized Cultural Heritage Artifacts from the Kingdom Era

Even as the revival of Shuri Castle provides a concrete image of the kingdom, it also makes apparent our significant loss of cultural heritage artifacts. That is to say, the restoration gave us the buildings, but the papers, various implements, works of art, and all the other items that would have been found therein remain unrecovered.

In the spring of 1609, the Satsuma forces occupied Shuri Castle for ten days and spent the time looting its treasures and sending them back to Kagoshima as spoils of war. In 1879, when the Meiji government abolished the kingdom and established Okinawa Prefecture, it seized a vast quantity of papers stored in Shuri Castle and moved them to Tokyo, where, tragically, they were destroyed in the catastrophic fires that followed the Great Kanto Earthquake of 1923. Faced with hard times after the collapse of the kingdom, members of Shuri's former elites sold their family heirlooms for low prices, and saw their legacies disappear into the markets of the Japanese mainland. Further, members of the victorious US military carried off large quantities of cultural items in the aftermath of the Battle of Okinawa. In short, during times of historic turbulence, many material objects that might convey the refinement and beauty of the kingdom era were swept away across the seas to distant lands. As a result, for example, some of the finest examples of Ryukyuan *raden*, lacquerware inlaid with mother-of-pearl, are to be found, not in Okinawa, but in the Boston Museum of Fine Arts in the United States. It is a tragedy of long standing that the people who are the inheritors of these kingdom-era cultural treasures have never even laid eyes on them directly.

Research into where these cultural artifacts might be found has begun only in recent years. It will take a considerable amount of time to grasp the overall picture of what remains of kingdom-era objects; attempts to borrow these items from the foreign museums and art galleries that hold them, to bring them home for exhibition, have barely started. The main point here, however, is that despite the restoration of the physical form of Shuri Castle, the fact is that the cultural assets of the Ryukyu Kingdom period are not in the hands of the prefectural residents to whom they rightly belong. This may be a heart-breaking acknowledgement, but it is an important starting point.

The Challenges of Conducting Research on the History of Ryukyu

In a sense, we can argue that the collapse of the Ryukyu Kingdom occurred only about a century ago. Despite this relatively short period of time, a majority of the tangible artifacts that attested to the kingdom's existence have vanished or have been dispersed outside the prefecture and overseas. Only a small fraction remains in our hands. Compounding this, the significance of the Ryukyu Kingdom's existence has been submerged and hidden by the ideology of Japan as a single, unified nation and ethnicity, and by dubious stories that obscure it even further.

Discussions about the Ryukyu Kingdom should be proud and

unashamedly assertive. In this, it is important not to become self-important; equally, we must avoid speaking from the perspective of people who have been victimized. In deepening our historical narrative about the Ryukyu Kingdom, we should take the stance that the work is not limited to questions about Ryukyuan history, but is also connected to enriching the narratives of Japanese and East Asian history.

To achieve this, the field of Ryukyuan history studies should not limit itself solely to the matter of Okinawan identity, but should instead strive continually to make universal representations that will also serve to reconstruct the historical narratives of Japan and East Asia. This is why I think centering Ryukyuan history on the story of the Ryukyu Kingdom has such great potential, and at the same time allows Okinawa, as an integral part of Japanese society with a unique regional character, to fulfill its responsibility of expressing those universal representations.

Postscript

At a time when I was overwhelmingly busy with the final stages of restoration work on Shuri Castle, and as a script supervisor and historical consultant for NHK's historical television drama *Ryūkyū no kaze* (Wind of the Ryukyu Islands), I also found myself obliged to write this book. To be honest, I had wanted an extension for submitting the manuscript, but my past record of breaking many deadline promises meant I had lost the right to any further concessions of extra time. How many times did I sigh deeply as I typed away on my keyboard? Given my lack of time, the inadequately polished draft of this book might have never seen the light of day had it not been for the meticulous work of Mr. Inoue Kazuo, my editor and first reader at Iwanami Shoten. In Okinawa, Mr. Inoue encouraged me over shared glasses of *awamori*, even as I caused him trouble with my lateness during the final stage of manuscript preparation. I take this opportunity to express my heartfelt gratitude to him.

Ryukyu's history remains relatively unknown, with even basic knowledge still not widely disseminated. As a historian, observing this makes me keenly aware of the inadequacies in our efforts.

This book is based on two previous volumes written with great ambitions, *Ryūkyū no jidai* (The Age of Ryukyu) and *Ryūkyū Ōkoku no kōzō* (The Structure of the Ryukyu Kingdom), with my life as a historian in Okinawa and my daily struggles to find answers adding another layer. While I drew on many research findings, I would like the reader to understand that due to the nature of this book, I could not mention every specific reference used.

POSTSCRIPT

Before engaging the main topic of Okinawan studies, there are many local matters that need to be addressed. As a historian, I feel the need to take part in resolving them. While I believe I have kept an objective historical perspective throughout this book, there may be places where I have fallen short in this. I welcome meticulous critique from readers on these shortcomings.

Takara Kurayoshi
December 1992
Twentieth anniversary of Okinawa's reversion to Japan

Historical Timeline for Ryukyu/Okinawa

Year	Era	Ryukyu/Okinawa	Japan	China, Korea, Southeast Asia
Approx. 30,000 years ago	Paleolithic era	Presumed *Homo sapiens*, Yamashita Cave Man (approx. 32,000 years ago) and Minatogawa Man (approx. 18,000 years ago).	Presumed *Homo sapiens*, Mikkabi Man, Hamakita Man (Shizuoka Prefecture), and Hijiridake Man (Ōita Prefecture).	
Approx. 5,000 years ago	Shell Mound era	Jōmon culture period begins.	Approx. 10,000–13,000 years ago, Jōmon culture period begins.	
		Differences from Japanese mainland increase over time, distinctive culture forms.	Yayoi culture	
Approx. 2,000 years ago		Evidence of Yayoi culture wave but estimated to have had no decisive impact.	Kofun culture	

HISTORICAL TIMELINE FOR RYUKYU/OKINAWA

Year	Era	Ryukyu/Okinawa	Japan	China, Korea, Southeast Asia
7th c.	Shell Mound era	No evidence of Kofun culture.	Japan sends envoy to Sui dynasty China (607).	
8th c.		First mention of "Liuqiuguo" (Liuqiu Kingdom) in *Book of Sui* section on eastern barbarians. Competing theories, such as Taiwan theory, Okinawa theory, and Compromise theory, no settled identification.	Capital established at Nara (710).	Sui dynasty collapses, Tang dynasty established (618).
		Buddhist monk Jianzhen (J. Ganjin) drifts ashore "Akonapa Island" (753 CE).	Capital established at Heian (Kyoto) (794).	
12th c.	Gusuku era	Full-scale agriculture begins, iron tool-use common. Local rulers known as *aji* emerge as political leaders, and *gusuku* fortifications widely constructed.	Minamoto no Yoritomo establishes *bakufu* capital at Kamakura (1192).	
13th c.		Yuan dynasty Chinese-Mongols raid Okinawa (1296 CE).		Chinese-Mongol Yuan dynasty launches military invasions of Japan (1274, 1281).

HISTORICAL TIMELINE FOR RYUKYU/OKINAWA

14th c.	Sanzan era	Sanzan (Three Mountains) era begins. Okinawa Island ruled by three powerful *aji* in separate domains: Sanhoku (Nakijin Castle), Chūzan (Urasoe Castle), and Sannan (Shimajiri Ōzato Castle, or Shimashii Ōzato Castle).	Ashikaga Takauji establishes Muromachi *bakufu* (1338).	Zhu Yuanzhang establishes Ming dynasty (1368).
1372		Envoys from Ming dynasty visit Ryukyu to urge its ruler to accept investiture and send tribute. King Satto of Chūzan accepts and dispatches younger brother Taiki as envoy. Kings of Sanhoku and Sannan follow suit, marking first exchanges of investiture and tribute and continues for 500 years. Chinese characters reading *Liuqiu* (J. Ryukyu) come into use.	*Wakō* pirates frequently raid Goryeo (Korean) coast.	
1389		King Satto also maintains relations with Goryeo (Korea).		
1392		First students sent from Ryukyu to study in Ming China.	Ashikaga Yoshimitsu accepts investiture envoys from Ming China and opens diplomatic relations (1401).	Sultanate of Malacca established around this time.

HISTORICAL TIMELINE FOR RYUKYU/OKINAWA

Year	Era	Ryukyu/Okinawa	Japan	China, Korea, Southeast Asia
1404	Sanzan era	First visit to Ryukyu by Ming envoys. Ships arrive from Siam for trade.	Licensed trade between Japan and China begins (1404).	Zhe He begins expeditions in South Pacific and Indian Ocean (1405–32).
1406		Shishō and son Shō Hashi attack Urasoe Castle, overthrow King Bunei of Chūzan, and seize throne. Capital of Chūzan presumably soon moves to Shuri Castle.	Ashikaga Yoshimochi severs relations with Ming China (1411).	Sultanate of Patani established on Malay Peninsula.
1416		Shō Hashi attacks and defeats Sanhoku's Nakijin Castle.		
1429	First Shō dynasty	Shō Hashi attacks and defeats Sannan's Shimashii Ōzato Castle. First Shō dynasty of Ryukyu Kingdom established with capital at Shuri Castle.		
1430		Trade and diplomatic relations with Java begin.		
1439		Quanzhou Ryukyu House, Rai'en'eki, established in Fujian Province.		

HISTORICAL TIMELINE FOR RYUKYU/OKINAWA

1456		Trade and diplomatic relations with Malacca begin.	
1458		Gosamaru-Amawari Rebellion	
		Ryukyu Kingdom reaches height of influence as it becomes transit-trade nation, dispatches trading ships to China, Japan, Korea, and Southeast Asia.	Ōnin War (1467–77)
1470	Second Shō dynasty	Coup d'état at Shuri Castle. Kanamaru installed on throne as King Shō En, establishes Second Shō dynasty.	
1472		Ryukyu House at Quanzhou moves to Jū'en'eki in Fuzhou.	
1477		Third king of Shō dynasty, King Shō Shin, accedes to throne.	
		During King Shō Shin's reign, Ryukyu Kingdom reaches greatest extent, stretching across vast ocean territory from Amami to Yaeyama.	

HISTORICAL TIMELINE FOR RYUKYU/OKINAWA

Year	Era	Ryukyu/Okinawa	Japan	China, Korea, Southeast Asia
1490	Second Shō dynasty	Trade and diplomatic relations with Patani begin.		
				Vasco de Gama arrives in Calcutta (Kolkata), India (1498).
1500		Akahachi-Hongawara Revolt in Yaeyama.		
				Portugal takes possession of Malacca (1511).
1531		First volume of *Omoro sōshi* compiled.		
			Heavy *wakō* pirate activity (Second *wakō* period).	
1542		Portuguese fleet visits Ryukyu.		
1543		Last trade ship voyages to Patani; trade with Southeast Asia declines.	Portuguese aboard Chinese ship drift ashore on Tanegashima (1543). First recorded Europeans to visit Japan.	Ming China allows Portuguese to reside in Macao (1557).
1570		Last trade ship sent to Siam. Trade with Southeast Asia ends.		
			Muromachi *bakufu* collapses (1573).	

HISTORICAL TIMELINE FOR RYUKYU/OKINAWA

1591	Toyotomi Hideyoshi demands troops and supplies for invasion into Korea.	Hideyoshi launches Korean invasion (Imjin War, 1592 and 1597).	
1609	Tokugawa Ieyasu gives permission for force of 3,000 soldiers from Satsuma to invade Ryukyu. Satsuma captures King Shō Nei and his ministers and takes control of Ryukyu (Shimazu Invasion).	Tokugawa Ieyasu establishes *bakufu* in Edo (Tokyo) (1603).	Japanese settlements established in various locations in Southeast Asia around this time.
	Kingdom's structure remains intact but incorporated into feudal *bakuhan* system in subordinate position. Era before Shimazu Invasion known as "ancient Ryukyu"; period after as "early modern Ryukyu."		
1624	Satsuma domain takes direct control of Amami islands.		
1634	First mission to Edo for accession of next shogun.		

HISTORICAL TIMELINE FOR RYUKYU/OKINAWA

Year	Era	Ryukyu/Okinawa	Japan	China, Korea, Southeast Asia
1637	Second Shō dynasty	Poll taxes levied on Sakishima (Miyako and Yaeyama islands).	Portuguese ships barred from entering port (1639).	Ming dynasty collapses. China reunified under Qing dynasty (1644).
1647		Government sugar monopoly established.		
1650		Shō Shōken (Haneji Chōshū) compiles *Chūzan seikan* (Mirror of Chūzan).		
1666		Shō Shōken becomes regent for King Shō Shitsu and works to rebuild nation.		
1701		Sai Taku compiles *Chūzan seifu* (Genealogy Book of Chūzan) (later revised).	Kyōhō Reforms	
1728		Sai On joins Council of Three (as first minister) and strives to stabilize nation.		

HISTORICAL TIMELINE FOR RYUKYU/OKINAWA

	Court culture flourishes, laying foundations for characteristic Ryukyuan (Okinawan) culture.		
1745	*Kyūyō* compiled.		
			First Opium War (1840–42)
1853	Commodore Perry arrives. Following First Opium War, foreign ships begin arriving in increasing numbers. In 1854, Perry returns and concludes Ryukyu-US Treaty of Amity.	Commodore Perry enters Uraga (located at entrance of Tokyo Bay) (1853). Japan-US Treaty of Amity signed following year.	
1866	Last imperial investiture envoy mission arrives in Ryukyu.	Meiji Restoration (1868) Abolition of *han* system and establishment of prefectures; Japan-China Treaty of Amity (1871).	Fifty-four people from Miyako killed when their ship drifts ashore on Taiwan (1871). This incident becomes pretext for Japan's invasion of Taiwan in 1874.
1872	Meiji government names King Shō Tai as lord of Ryukyu domain.		

HISTORICAL TIMELINE FOR RYUKYU/OKINAWA

Year	Era	Ryukyu/Okinawa	Japan	China, Korea, Southeast Asia
1874	Second Shō dynasty	Last tribute ship dispatched to China.		
1879	Okinawa Prefecture	Meiji government abolishes Ryukyu domain and establishes Okinawa Prefecture (Disposition of Ryukyu). Meiji government mobilizes military and police to force surrender of Shuri Castle, and relocation of King Shō Tai to Tokyo. Ryukyu Kingdom collapses 450 years after founding.		Former US president Grant mediates negotiations for division of Ryukyu between Qing China and Japan, (Negotiations for island division and expansion of [US] presence, 1880).
1903		Sakishima poll taxes abolished.		
1945	US military governance	Battle of Okinawa. Estimated 200,000 Okinawan civilians killed.	Japan accepts Potsdam Declaration and agrees to total surrender.	
1972	Okinawa Prefecture	Reversion to Japanese sovereignty, becomes Okinawa Prefecture again.		

Key References

This list is limited to fundamental single-volume works that complement the narrative of this book; collections of historical materials have been omitted. The focus is also restricted to the period centered around ancient (medieval) Ryukyu.

Akiyama Kenzō. *Nis-Shi kōshōshi kenkyū* [Research on the History of Sino-Japanese Cultural Interactions]. Tokyo: Iwanami Shoten, 1939.

Araki Moriaki. *Shin Okinawashi ron* [New History of Okinawa Theory]. Naha: Okinawa Times, 1980.

Asato Susumu. *Kōkogaku kara mita Ryūkyūshi* [The History of Ryukyu from an Archaeological Perspective]. 2 vols. Naha: Hirugisha, 1990–91.

Higa Minoru. *Ko Ryūkyū no shisō* [The Thought of Ancient Ryukyu]. Naha: Okinawa Times, 1991.

Higashionna Kanjun. *Higashionna Kanjun zenshū 3* [The Complete Works of Higashionna Kanjun 3]. Tokyo: Daiichi Shobō, 1979. First published in 1941 as *Reimeiki no kaigai kōtsūshi* [The Early History of Maritime Transportation] by Teikoku Kyōikukai Shuppanbu.

Ifa Fuyū. *Ko Ryūkyū no seiji* [The Politics of Ancient Ryukyu]. Vol. 1 of *Ifa Fuyū zenshū* [The Complete Works of Ifa Fuyū], edited by Hattori Shirō, Nakasone Seizen, and Hokama Shuzen. Tokyo: Heibonsha, 1974.

Kamiya Nobuyuki. *Bakuhansei kokka no Ryūkyū shihai* [Governance of Ryukyu under the State Feudal System]. Tokyo: Azekura Shobō, 1990.

Kishino Hisashi. *Seiōjin no Nihon hakken: Zabieru rainichizen Nihon jōhō no kenkyū* [Discovery of Japan by Western Europeans: Research on Information about Japan before Xavier's Arrival]. Tokyo: Yoshikawa Kōbunkan, 1989.

Kobata Atsushi. *Zōho chūsei nantō tsūkō bōekishi no kenkyū* [Research on the History of Medieval South Island Trade and Exchange, enlarged ed.]. Tokyo: Tōkō Shoin, 1968.

Murai Shōsuke. *Ajia no naka no chūsei Nihon* [Medieval Japan in Asia]. Tokyo: Azekura Shobō, 1988.

Ryukyu Shinpo Editorial, ed. *Shin Ryūkyūshi* [New History of Ryukyu]. *Ko Ryūkyū hen* [Ancient Ryukyu Series]. Naha: Ryūkyū Shinpō, 1991.

Sakuma Shigeo. *Nichi-Min kankeishi no kenkyū* [Research on Japan-Ming Relations History]. Tokyo: Yoshikawa Kōbunkan, 1992.

Takara Kurayoshi. *Ryūkyū Ōkokushi no kadai* [Issues in the History of the Ryukyu Kingdom]. Naha: Hirugisha, 1989.

———. *Ryūkyū no jidai* [The Age of Ryukyu]. Tokyo: Chikuma Shobō, 2012.

———. *Ryūkyū Ōkoku no kōzō* [The Structure of the Ryukyu Kingdom]. Tokyo: Yoshikawa Kōbunkan, 1987.

———. *Shinpan Ryūkyū no jidai: Ōinaru rekishizō o motomete* [New Edition, The Age of Ryukyu: Seeking a Grand View of History]. Naha: Hirugisha, 1989.

Tanaka Takeo. *Chūsei taigai kankeishi* [A History of Medieval Foreign Relations]. Tokyo: University of Tokyo Press, 1975.

———. *Taigai kankei to bunka kōryū* [Foreign Relations and Cultural Exchange]. Kyoto: Shibunkaku Publishing, 1982.

———. *Wakō: Umi no rekishi* [Pirates: History of the Seas]. Tokyo: Kyoikusha, 1982.

About the Author and Translator

Takara Kurayoshi is professor emeritus at the University of the Ryukyus. He received his BA in Ryukyuan history from Aichi University of Education and his PhD from Kyushu University. He has been a specialist at the Okinawa Historical Materials Editorial Office, director of Urasoe City Library, chief examiner at Okinawa Prefectural Museum & Art Museum, and executive director of The Okinawa History Research Society. A native of Okinawa, he was born on Izena Island in 1947 and raised on the island of Minamidaitōjima. He has written and contributed to many works on Ryukyu, including *Ryūkyū Ōkoku no kōzō* [The Structure of the Ryukyu Kingdom] (Yoshikawa Kōbunkan, 1987); *Ajia no naka no Ryūkyū Ōkoku* [The Ryukyu Kingdom in Asia] (Yoshikawa Kōbunkan, 1998); *Ryūkyū Ōkokushi no tankyū* [Quest for the Ryukyu Kingdom's History] (Gajumaru Shorin, 2011); and *Ryūkyū no jidai* [The Age of Ryukyu] (Chikuma Shobō, 2012).

Lina Terrell is a program coordinator and instructor at Austin Community College in Austin, Texas. She received her BA in East Asian studies from the College of William & Mary (1988), an MA in applied linguistics from The University of Texas at Austin (1996), and an MA in Japanese historical linguistics from the University of Hawai'i at Mānoa (2009). Previous Japanese-to-English translated works include Takazawa Kōji's *Destiny: The Secret Operations of the Yodogō Exiles* (University of Hawai'i Press, 2017) and Akamine Mamoru's *The Ryukyu Kingdom: Cornerstone of East Asia* (University of Hawai'i Press, 2016).

(英文版) 琉球王国
The Legacy of the Ryukyu Kingdom: An Okinawan History

2025年3月27日　第1刷発行

著　者　　高良倉吉
訳　者　　リナ・テレル
企　画　　公益財団法人日本国際問題研究所
発行所　　一般財団法人出版文化産業振興財団
　　　　　〒101-0051 東京都千代田区神田神保町2-2-30
　　　　　電話　03-5211-7283
　　　　　ホームページ　https://www.jpic.or.jp/

印刷・製本所　　大日本印刷株式会社

定価はカバーに表示してあります。
本書の無断複写(コピー)、転載は著作権法の例外を除き、禁じられています。

© 1993 Takara Kurayoshi
Printed in Japan
hardcover ISBN 978-4-86658-258-0
ebook (ePub) ISBN 978-4-86658-259-7
ebook (PDF) ISBN 978-4-86658-260-3